A Matter of Identity

A life recalled in poetry

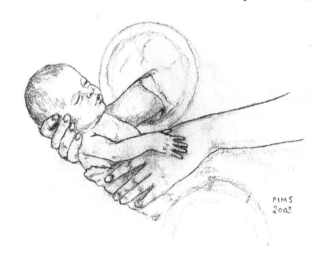

MMS
2003

MARGARET SPARSHOTT

A MATTER OF IDENTITY

"Who is the Lord to whom I pray?
Without knowing, what can I say?
So -
Have you any suggestion?"

No!
You must answer the question.

Margaret Sparshott,
July 2003

Dedication

This book is dedicated to John and Elizabeth,
friends of many years.

Thanks

To my sister Elizabeth, for her support and encouragement; to my brother Francis, for permission to use his photograph for the drawing of my mother, and allowing me to quote his poem; to the communities of Lee Abbey and Noddfa, and the Community of St. Francis at Compton Durville for the refuge and refreshment they offer; to Helen and Rob for the hospitality of Hampton Manor. My thanks also to everyone met during a long lifetime; the friends and acquaintances who people the poems, all of whom have taught me the stuff of living.

CONTENTS

Cover design by Stamford House Publishing

Photograph 'Beach at Lee Bay' by the author

Pencil drawings by the author

Introduction

Many people see their lives as a 'pilgrim's progress'; a journey up hill and down dale, across bogs, streams, rivers and oceans, through fields and forests, cities and slums, sometimes happy, sometimes sad – sometimes despairing. But always onward, body and spirit together. My life (and perhaps yours too) has been a journey of this kind.

On the way there are many questions to be asked, and relatively few answers to be given. How do we understand the people we meet, what they think and feel – and believe? What exists in the matter of animals, birds, trees and plants, things which live in the world but apart from us, equally alive, but different? How do we identify pain and delight, sorrow and joy in all these things? Who are you – who am I – if there is a Creator God, who and what is He? All these are matters of identity; but to me, my own identity seems not entirely my own. How am I to understand why I do the things I do, and feel the things I feel?

A few months ago I decided to turn out the hoards of papers I have accumulated over the years; there are files full to bursting, and, reluctant as I am to let anything go (because who knows? old books of study notes from the 1950s might come in handy some day!) space in my attic is limited. So I sat on my spare room floor and gutted the files one by one. Many things went into the wastepaper basket, but here and there I turned up poems I have written over the years – some are hand written on paper yellow with age. On this discovery I gladly abandoned the rest of the clearance, and set myself to sort the poems into seasons.

My memory of when I first began to write poetry is dim. It is rather like trying to recall the first sensation of pain; the first remembered pain cannot have been the first experience. 'Distraction' is a form of pain treatment, and many of the poems must be responses to some deeply felt contemporary anxiety or concern. Others seem to express deeply felt joy and exhilaration. Sifting through these poems, trying to put them in some sort of order, led me to remember the pains and pleasures of a very diverse lifetime.

The question "How do I know what I feel until I hear what I say?" makes a relevant introduction to this book and the poems within it, which seem to reflect different stages of my life, though many are undated and I cannot know exactly when and why they were written. As I read them now and look back to then, perhaps they will help me understand my own personal journey.

I had a Christian upbringing, and although belief has wavered and grown thin from time to time, the faith I grew up with has never quite left me; now in retirement, when life has fewer distractions and is less busy, belief in a loving God has helped to sustain me, and is the source of many of the poems I have chosen here. I find that by writing and drawing I can liberate things that lie deep, and that I hold dear – how hard it is to speak of such things! But they can be written and drawn.

PART I:

FIRST THINGS

Rochester, Lamberhurst, Taunton and Sidmouth

Rochester, Lamberhurst, Taunton and Sidmouth

I was fortunate in having a happy childhood; I never doubted that my father and mother loved each other and that they loved me. Love within a family during early years is a blessing that can never be taken away, no matter what happens later, but perhaps this is something one realises only towards the end of life, when one looks back and sees the pattern and meaning of what has gone before.

I was born on a Thursday; the rhyme says that Thursday's children have 'far to go' and indeed I have spent much of my life travelling. To begin with this was due to the changes wartime brought to my family, but later I developed a desire to see for myself what is going on in the rest of the world - and perhaps also there was a latent taste for risk. Circumstances led me in different directions; to be always in one place makes me restless. I was five years old when war broke out, and eleven when it finished, and it may be because of these early moves with my family (which at the time I was very happy with) that I have never put down roots.

My father was a schoolmaster, Head of the Junior School of King's School, Rochester. At the outbreak of war my family was evacuated with the boys to Scotney Castle in Lamberhurst. My father was in charge of the boys, my mother 'kept house' for us all, my sister Elizabeth, ten years older than I am, was given a year off school to act as Under Matron, and my brother Francis was a pupil at the Senior School which had been evacuated to Bayham Abbey nearby.

Scotney Castle was a wonderful playground for a five year old little girl; everyone was too busy to keep me in sight, and I ran wild in the gardens and park, and explored the earth-smelling Home Woods; always a walk in wet woodland will recall the untamed smell of them. Then after a year, because of the potential danger from German aircraft jettisoning their bombs on their way back to the Channel, we were moved again to Taunton, where the King's School and Eltham College were combined with Taunton School for the rest of the war. In Taunton, the boys were boarded with the Junior School so the family lived in a rented house nearby.

From an early age I was encouraged to read. My sister Elizabeth gave me my first book of poetry for Christmas when I was ten years old; it was Walter de la Mare's anthology *'Come Hither'*, and I have it still, worn and well fingered, sixty-two years later. As I was sitting by the fire with the new book in my hands, she suggested I read Coleridge's *'Rhyme of the Ancient Mariner'*, but reading it horrified me so much I became for a short time unable to move. It was the thought of the mariner slaying the albatross, and then being compelled to wear the dead bird hanging from a cord round his neck, that shocked me so.

Elizabeth would also read Shakespeare's plays with me, allowing me to perform all the meaty parts; it was a wonderful way to give a child a love for words. She encouraged me to appreciate paintings, and to develop a talent for drawing; while we were still in Taunton she gave me my first book on World Art, which I loved at the time but sadly have long since lost.

When I was a little girl, Father also would read to me before I went to sleep; but best he loved to tell stories. He had a gift for cartoon-style drawing, and as he described the fantastic and funny adventures of Sammy Slope, who every night would climb from his bedroom window and escape on a moonbeam,

6

he would illustrate them by quick little sketches. He had no talent for writing, but my sister tells me she used to creep up the stairs after I had been put to bed, and sit outside the door to listen to him.

After the war was over, we returned to Rochester. From Rochester, Father loved to take us up to London on the train for days of exploration; he delighted in showing his children the things that interested him, and so he infected us too with his enthusiasm. We went to the theatre, the ballet, and the opera, and we visited the museums and the art galleries, and to this day I still like to spend time when in London going to see old favourites; the Victoria and Albert and British Museums and the National Gallery are much-loved, but there is still a stuffed and shabby tiger in the Natural History Museum, which I would swear was gathering dust there fifty years ago.

When I was fifteen, Father was beginning to be affected by the degenerative brain disease now known as Altzheimer's, and could no longer think clearly. He was still in his fifties, and had to retire early, quite incapable of teaching. My mother took him to Sidmouth, where they bought a house, and thus began the long love affair of my family for Devon.

The following three poems seem relevant to this part of my life. There are two of the earliest poems I have kept over the years, and one by my brother, the only one in this book that I have not written myself.

POEMS

'*A Case of Psychasthenia in a School Teacher*' was written by my brother Francis. It is about my father, and I have included it in this book because it expresses far better than I ever could the tragedy attached to that condition.

A CASE OF PSYCHASTHENIA IN A SCHOOL TEACHER

During the first year he would stand bewildered,
Speechless. The children roared,
Buffeted him. At evening he went home,
Told no one. At last they found him.

In the second year the wards received him,
Drugs shocked and soothed. He fell sick,
Nearly died, but his strength saved him.
He was helpful around the wards, but nothing could be done
For him, he went home.

In the third year he was given a testimonial and
Left the county, to plant beans and lettuce;
Read novels, greeted his friends
Loudly and cheerfully by the wrong names.

In the fourth year he could not remember
How potatoes are planted; muttered, hummed cheerlessly,
Snapped his fingers; if left alone
Would bicycle through the town, searching till he fell
Fainting. Strangers brought him home.

In the fifth year he could neither read nor
Chat; lay long abed. His weakness
Grew beyond woman's helping; strength stayed
Past guidance. The wards received him.

In the sixth year the wards held him.
He did not look for his wife if she could not come;
If she came, he knew. He sickened, nearly died,
But his strength saved him.
His last word was yes.

In the seventh year his son made these verses.
Thinking this useful knowledge: what may come
To a gentle and good man, loved by many,
Who had worked long and painfully for small reward;

Thinking it right, too, to proclaim
A wife's endurance
Who with patient care and without hope tended
Her husband's grave
For those years till the wards received him.

Francis Sparshott. From: A Divided Voice, Toronto Oxford University Press, 1965

'Rain in a Chinese Picture' is the first poem I remember writing. One of the pictures in the book on World Art that Elizabeth gave me was a Chinese painting representing rain slanting across a wall, over which can be seen only the tops of trees and the tower of a pagoda, from which hangs a bell. Though beautiful, it seemed to me a sad painting; I don't recall the name of the artist, but now, reading the poem, I remember the picture.

RAIN IN A CHINESE PICTURE

By the monastery garden
The rain falls –
Spears of white light falling
From a mud-coloured sky.
By the monastery garden
The rain falls
Striking the roadway with a solid sound.
Rain on the asphalt
Has a maddening sound
As persistent and relentless as machine-gun fire.
Here the rain is angry.
But inside the garden
The rain falls
Gently, mournfully,
Touching the greenery
With caressing hands.
Here the leaves droop,
The branches droop,
And the rain falls from the leaves and branches,
From the roof-tops and the eaves
Where the bell hangs mutely,
So sodden, that it seems
Impossible
That it should ever ring again.

Margaret Sparshott

'The Lonely Woodland' was written much later. At the time I was working at St. Thomas' Hospital in London as a student nurse, and would spend my holidays at home in Sidmouth. In spite of his illness Father still loved the country, and we would walk up to Peak Hill along a stretch of new plantation called Mutters Moor. Then, the trees were still young and growing, and in fine weather there was a wonderful view to the West. I wrote 'The Lonely Woodland' following one solitary walk on this ridge, when I was suddenly overwhelmed by mist creeping in from the sea.

THE LONELY WOODLAND

They that dwelt in the woods are gone,
And there is now only
A songless silence
Where the pine is withered and the bracken is burnt
Over the hill-crests.
They that dwelt in the woods
Have stolen from the woods their mystery,
And their cold altars bleach beneath the sun.
The woods are lonely.
But when the light rain falls on an Autumn dusk,
Bending the pine-boughs and greying the grass,
Perhaps the dryad sits
Listening among the branches, and the nymph
Dips her pale fingers in the wet heather.
Do they return then?
Perhaps they drift in with the mist from the sea,
Or perhaps
They rise timid out of the ground,
Or perhaps they form
Eerily out of the air,
To linger sadly in their former haunts
And play forgotten music on their broken reeds.
But with the first touch of the sun
They that dwelt in the woods are gone.

Margaret Sparshott

PART II:

LONDON & SHREWSBURY

Church, Hospital, and the Bank of England

Church

When I left school I went to work in London. During this time I attended All Souls' Church, Langham Place, but more from habit than conviction. My parents and sister were all church-going Christians of strong faith; but although it never entirely left me, my own faith was more dutiful than warm. During the Fifties the Evangelist Billy Graham came to England on one of his soul saving missions. He was a great friend of the Reverend John Stott, and I was for a time caught up in the enthusiastic spirit.

From the years in London date the earliest of the religious poems I have continued to write at various stages during my life. Some of them seem to me now derivative, some naïve, some have the gloom and doom of youth and inexperience, but they were heartfelt, and they do represent a period of my life which, while not unhappy, I remember as being an anxious time. It is never comfortable to be different, and my understanding of the Bible was unlike that of my peers at All Souls', who held that Christians must believe the Bible word for word, and blow by blow – and there are a good many blows in the Old Testament! Perhaps, I thought then, I wasn't a genuine Christian, and my belief in Jesus and redemption for all men was just an emotion, a warm cuddly feeling that existed only on the surface. Or perhaps I was guilty of an intellectual snobbery, in finding the beliefs of my peers too simplistic, even comical. So I was uneasy with myself. My father, who was a devout man and a wise one, might have been able to help me, but he had already become ill and was no longer capable of thinking.

The first six poems in this section reflect the unease prevalent at that time, and my unease at the direction my own life was taking. *'A Bloody Christmas'*, and *'Fall'*, clearly refer to IRA violence, war, and pollution; it interests me to see in 'Fall' that I have remembered the albatross in the image of birds falling under the bow, and the bunches of tattered and tumbled feathers.

POEMS

A BLOODY CHRISTMAS

Now softly, softly quilts the snow
The poisoned land;
Thinly the firelight filters through
The wasted hand.

Now gently, gently sleeps the babe
That cannot wait,
Though warmly wrapped and richly fed,
To grow – and hate.

The wise men come from foreign lands
And they despise
All those who look upon the world
With alien eyes.

Hunger, contempt and violence,
These wise three
Have come together at a strange
Nativity.

No-one gains from a shining star;
The mystic birth
To a greedy world is a poor exchange
For riches on earth.

The city of God is for those who kill,
And do not stay
Beside the bombs to see whose flesh
Is torn away.

What do they care for a bloody cross?
The failing breath
Can never move those whose pitiless hearts
Are set on death.

Meaningless now the scattered shroud,
The empty grave;
Joyless the feast of blood and flesh
That cannot save.

Bread and wine, wine and bread
Are nothing at all,
To those who kill, but blood and flesh
Sprayed on a wall.

Margaret Sparshott

FALL

I see the trees falling
  And falling and falling.
I see the trees falling
  Under the blade.
And here are the brambles,
The dust and the desert;
The dust of the desert
  That offers no shade.

I see the birds falling
  And falling and falling.
I see the birds falling
  Under the bow.
And what should I find
In these bunches of feathers
That tumbled and tattered
  Lie staining the snow?

I see the earth falling
  And falling and falling.
I see the earth falling
  Under the plough.
None but the gulls
That wheel over and over
Can look to the furrows
  For sustenance now.

I see the streets falling
  And falling and falling.
I see the streets falling
  Under the shells.
But what should I find

In the heaps of dry rubble
That emptily echo
   The tolling of bells?

The hammer is falling
   And falling and falling.
The hammer is falling
   On nails in His hands.
I see the tears falling
And blinding the people
Silent on Golgotha
   Where the Tree stands.

I see the Tree falling.
Margaret Sparshott

The drawing of the Riven Head which accompanies *'A Vision of the Cross'* is a copy of a wooden carving in the Finnish Folk Museum in Helsinki. This was drawn long after I wrote the poem, but seems to fit. I was in Helsinki for a conference on paediatric pain when I came across the head, leaning modestly in a corner against a wall, and was struck by its calm beauty. The crack is a natural one, caused by shrinkage of the wood, but it seems very appropriate under the crown of thorns.

A VISION OF THE CROSS

'A man of sorrows and acquainted with grief' -
   Can this be He
Who rode in triumph to Jerusalem,
   Nailed to a tree?

As I walk up the hillside
   Carrying the Cross,
Bitter the agony of shame,
   Bitter the loss.

The stones beneath me are sharp and hot,
   Cutting my feet;
They carry upon themselves a trail of blood
   Behind in the street.

A dusty wind blows in my face
   Blinding my eyes –
Yet I can see the shape of Golgotha
   Against the skies.

The Riven Head

Brother, has sin so blinded you?
  I ask you to see
That you must now carry your own Cross
  And follow me.

Sister, however weary your heart,
  Heavy your load;
I am the Way. Follow me – there is
  No other road.

Brother and sister both,
  Dearest and best,
You must take my yoke upon you –
  And you shall have rest.
Margaret Sparshott

Strangely, I have no clear recollection of what was disturbing me when I wrote the poems '*And Great was the Fall of It*', and *'The Follower'*, though I must have been unhappy; it may have been disbelief at the breaking of a loving but very difficult relationship. How strange not to remember what must have been a very strong emotion, so long ago! But the passing years have changed my way of thinking – closed doors don't have to remain closed. I believe now that one should never let oneself be overcome by a fall - even if the frailty which led to it should never be forgotten but accepted as something to be wary of life-long.

Perhaps this is why I find books about little, weak people, struggling to live good lives against all hope, so satisfying. I think particularly of J.R.R.Tolkien's *'Lord of the Rings'* and the small and insignificant hobbits taking the road that leads on and ever on: *'A great dread fell upon [Frodo]... At last with an effort he spoke, and wondered to hear his own words, as if some other will was using his small voice. "I will take the Ring," he said, "though I do not know the way."'*

The next poem must stand by the first three verses because that is how it was written, but that was then. After rediscovering it, I completed the last verse in 2004; this was now.

AND GREAT WAS THE FALL OF IT

I built a house for shelter,
I built it upon the sand,
And the rains came and the winds blew
Across the barren land –
And the heat of the desert burnt it
With the rage of the desert sun;
And great was the fall of roof and wall
  As they tumbled, one by one.

I built a house for shelter,
I built it upon the shore
With the cliffs erect behind it
And the gulls a-wheel before –
But who can command the tempest?
The wind and the waves are free,
So great was the fall of roof and wall
  Beside the devouring sea.

I built a house for shelter,
I built it upon the rock,
And I hear a voice say gently, "Lo,
I stand at the door and knock."
But I slam the door and I shoot the bolt,
And I make no answer at all.
For I know that the rock will heave and split
  And again, my house must fall.

I built a house for shelter;
I built it long ago.
Oh if only I knew when I built it
The things that now I know!
But the rock on which I built my house
Is still and ever a rock;

Jesus of Hetteral Ridge
Statue by Roseanne Keller in
Exeter Cathedral

And still in the night I hear that voice,
"I am here at your door, I knock."
Now I perceive, after the years,
This rock built house must stand,
If I hear the knock, and I hear the voice,
  And I take that outstretched hand.
                    Margaret Sparshott

THE FOLLOWER

Has my God deserted me
  That I loved in the days
When childhood was at hand with me
  And walked the tangled ways,
When God was God and nothing less
  As real as earth and air?
Now I am lost in loneliness
  Is He no longer there?

Has he turned his face from me
  Whom once I thought my friend
And left me comfortless to see
  Confusion to the end?
Has He ignored my groping hand,
  Not listened when I pray,
Will He not lead me through this night
  Towards a brighter day?

I must believe I have Him still
  Beyond and far above –
Forgive me Lord – I cannot kill,
  I cannot kill my love.
                    Margaret Sparshott

I have always been fascinated by the story of the raising of *'Lazarus'*; what can he have felt about it all? Did he have an after death experience and remember what had happened to him between his death and resurrection? It seems hard that he should come to life only to die again - was he in fact violently put to death the second time, as was threatened? We are not told the end of the story.

LAZARUS

Once more from this catacomb that contained my soul –
　Tight and small, enclosing a blind and breathless heat –
I behold the bright sky, curved like a round bowl.
　I hear once again the trample of many feet
Raising dust-feathers from the threshing floor;
　Hear voices, all amazed, recalling me.
　And one Voice calling that I knew before –
Love calls me to return! No longer free
　But held in bondage to a terrible trust.
Love calls me to return! I must
Forget the half-seen Kingdom of my dream.
　And yet, and yet – whilst flesh warms in the sun –
The cool, swift winds of Heaven, how near they seem!
　My soul will not be still – I rise! I run!

What need have I to drink wine and break bread;
　For am I not the living, I alone amongst the dead?

Margaret Sparshott

Hospital

In London I worked first as a shorthand typist living in a girls' hostel in Mortimer Street, but after a lot of lazy prevarication I decided to follow up a childhood love for nursing. So, at the age of twenty-one, I entered St. Thomas' Hospital as a student nurse, and there I remained for the next four years.

Nursing was a shock to me. Like many others before me, I had seen myself as smoothing brows and pillows, and being admired by all the poor sick people I was about to cure. Instead, there was vomit and stench and pain, and constant admonishment from Ward Sisters for being too slow. The poem *'Night Duty, St. Thomas' Hospital'*, which I wrote in 1996, is a recollection of one single night, but there were many other nights like it.

After I had completed my nursing and midwifery training, I worked in Shrewsbury, in order to be near my family. My brother Francis had left England for Canada at the age of twenty-one; my father was in a psychiatric hospital no longer able to talk, and my mother was living with and looking after my sister Elizabeth, who was Headmistress of a school in Ludlow.

I worked as a Staff Nurse on a women's medical ward, and there made the acquaintance of the nurse who was for a brief time to become my best friend. She is the subject of the poem: *'This Message is for You, my Gentle Friend'*. She was still working as a nurse, but was beginning to be handicapped by the genetic illness that was later to kill her. She was a wonderful friend; we were in fact twins, same age, same birthday, and we liked the same books, admired the same film stars (James Mason, Gary Cooper) – we were always talking

31

and laughing. The laughter never ceased, but gradually she ceased to be a nurse and became a patient. Not long after that she became too weak to breathe, and so died. At the time I wrote the poem I could not remember her name, but of course thinking about her brought it back to me – it was Barbara.

Later that same day I was on duty and in charge of the ward. Since there was no one to replace me, I had to prepare her body for death ('laying out the body' they called it), and could only be helped by a senior student nurse – there was no one else. This was her first experience of death, and of course she also knew Barbara and was distressed. At the time I resented this obligation, but now I see that it was not such a bad thing; the student nurse and I moved gently and talked quietly, and I was left with a feeling that preparing a body after death is a last service one can offer a person – making things good. I was to feel this many years later when my sister and I performed the same service for our mother, which I also recorded in the poem, which appears later in this book, '*Our Mother Died*'.

POEMS

NIGHT DUTY, ST. THOMAS' HOSPITAL:
Winter, 1958

The dark ward at night.
The nurse, under the light,
The white-capped centre of a web whose strands
Stretch left to the dim-bulbed entrance, right
To the balcony door.
Slow-flowing, the river winds
Through Westminster. Big Ben strikes four;
Now is the time for dying –
But no-one dies tonight.

This is no place of rest.
The patients fidget, like fledglings in a nest
Foiled in flying;
They rustle and cough, moan and sigh.
She takes the torch and makes her way
Past the sick sleepers. 'Nurse' cries one –
Two eyes caught in the beam
Plead for a basic need; the nurse
Hurries to the icy sluice
For the clattering pan,
Hands fumbling numb.
She swills a sheet and hangs it on the balcony
To stiffen with excrement and frost.

Here's no romance, adventure, drama to excite;
Only the hourly vigil to repeat.
Personal feelings, dreams, and aims are lost
When slow and weary feet

Tread creaking boards on monotonous patrol;
Responding to the call of nature, and the call
For sleep, and the cry of pain, and the tears of weakness, all
Through the endless, cold and lonely night.

Margaret Sparshott:
First published in 'The NHS Experience'
Anchor Books, 1996

THIS POEM IS FOR YOU, MY GENTLE FRIEND

This poem is for you, my gentle friend,
Whose name I have forgotten.

We were twenty-one,
Born in the same year,
On the same day,
At the same hour,
We met each other first
When my life could be said
Scarcely to have begun.
Yours was already ending –
This we both knew.

Lurching on stiff hips
And never without pain,
You could still laugh when
We told jokes, sang songs,
Dreamed of the same handsome men
We loved but never met.
We laughed at our dreams – although we knew that yours
Were fruitless dreams indeed.

I held your hand when you gasped for life,
Your forceful brain refusing to condone
Your disobedient body.
O you were too aware!
You saw your death in my tears,
But to my grief and shame,
Your eyes held no reproach.
How could I hurt you so?
I had forgotten, long ago,
Your eyes, your touch – your stare, your clutch –
Now, I forget your name.

Margaret Sparshott:
First published in: 'Forever Friends',
Triumph House, 1999

Since writing this poem I have remembered her name – it was Barbara

The Bank of England

The last poems in this section were written during the six years I worked in London before going to Greece. Three of those years I worked in Devonshire Street as Ward Sister of the Chest Wards of University College Hospital, and for three years I was a nurse at the Bank of England in Threadneedle Street. While I was there I experienced a normal social life for the first time since starting nursing, and enjoyed myself enormously, writing and drawing for competitions, which I won, and acting in the Dramatic Society plays, for which I had my name engraved for posterity on a silver cup! I lived in a bed-sitter in Belsize Park, travelled to and from work on the Northern line, and had many friends who had nothing whatever to do with the medical profession. It was a glorious change and I relished those three years very much.

When I was in London, there was a 'Coffee House' society, which seems very innocent from this distance in time; but we thought we were very daring! One wore jeans and duffle coat, had long hair and masses of eyeshadow and mascara, smoked incessantly and talked non-stop.

The first Coffee House ever, as far as I know, was in Northumberland Avenue, and the last time I went down to Trafalgar Square, there it still was. I belonged to a little group of mixed bag; a couple of shorthand typists, two actors and an actress, two BBC producers, and Marcel the amorous Frenchman. The Coffee House society ran a little journal, which liked to shock, and the first poem *'Orpheus'* was written for this – but was not thought shocking enough. So then I wrote another one, a copy of which I have conveniently lost.

POEMS

ORPHEUS

Looking into your eyes, I see
Myself reflected
Swan-mirrored,
Pluto-deep in the pit.
We are prisoners, you and I,
I in you and you in me;
For us there is no escape.
Even tenderness at nightfall,
Soft-fingered love at dusk,
Light-fingers of love at nightfall,
Cannot release the soul from bondage.

Could we escape, Eurydice,
And run together up the dark road,
Turning only to look through the bars with pity,
We would be gods indeed, and rule eternity together –

But for us there is no escape.
Margaret Sparshott, London

'Aldemaston' and 'The Magic Box' were written in the 'swinging sixties', which never affected me very much. I am a little ashamed now of ridiculing the Aldemaston marchers, but I have to put the poems in because they were fun to write (even if serious in context) and to leave them out would not be fair to this book's title: 'A Matter of Identity'. And I have not changed much; I still mistrust demonstrating crowds (some participants have their own agenda), and dislike the sense of being controlled by the media.

ALDEMASTON

Chorus
Glory, glory Aldemaston
Not so glorious as the past'n
Now they tell us it's the last'n,
But we'll still go marching on.

I'm an honest politician, and I'm called a man of reason.
I've been on all these marches, and 'sat down' in every season.
I'm prepared to sell state secrets, but you couldn't call it

treason,
So I still go marching on.

I'm an angry playwright, but my anger's rather blunt,
And since my days of mutiny I've had a change of front;
So now I must admit I do the whole thing for a stunt,
And I go marching on.

I'm a bearded student, but I don't know what I study;
My face is cold, my knees are wet, my feet are very muddy,
And now I must confess I find the whole thing rather bloody
But I still go marching on.

I'm a good old Communist, and I must worm my way
Into everybody's confidence, and hear what people say.
Ban the bomb! My poor young comrades, that'll be the day!
And I go marching on.

I'm a nice young parson, but I can't be very bright;
I try hard to express myself – I try to do what's right.
Why is it that my honest sermons always sound so trite
As I go marching on?

I'm a little actress and I really think I care;
I've a duffle coat and blue jeans, and I've long untidy hair,
So other girls can see and say "I wonder how she dare?"
So I go marching on.

I'm an old philosopher – I don't believe in God –
So you might think my presence here upon this dreary plod
Neither logical nor rational, but just extremely odd,
Yet I still go marching on!

A lot I care for scientist! To hell with bloody parson!
And I don't much care for bloody bombs – I'm on the run for
                                                            arson,
Now all I want's a bloody gate to rest my bloody arse on –
You can keep your marching on!

I am an honest pacifist, and as I march today
I know I've got an argument – yet everything I say
And do seems so inadequate – but there's no other way –
I must go marching on.

I am a human onlooker – I think that I know why
They're marching – but it's useless; I wonder that they try.
And anyway, considering all, I think I'd rather die.
So I'm not marching on.

Glory, glory Aldemaston, etc....

Margaret Sparshott, London.

39

THE MAGIC BOX

Come you little children, come and gather round,
I want to show the secret of a magic box I've found.
Come on, you've nothing else to do, you can't play in the
                                                    street,
And Mum and Dad are fed up with you always round their feet.
Perhaps they're going to join in too, they're going to share the
                                                    fun;
You needn't fear that you'll be bored, there's lots for everyone.

Look, here's a football hooligan, beating up his brother,
And here are two policemen, swearing at each other;
Press the switch, and let us see what new delights I've found –
The weekly play, a couple making love upon the ground!
Oh, sorry! That's supposed to be just for the late at night
When all good little kiddiwinks are wrapped up sleepy-tight.

Here's a famous pop-star – let me hear you shriek –
Girls go convulsive at the sight of this illuminated freak;
The really 'cool' can faint away – do you want to be behind?
Hysteria gets a day off school and no-one's going to mind.
Here's a war film, lovely stuff with corpses in the mud
And all the nasty Nazis are wallowing in the blood.

Here's a Mum whose daughter has been murdered in a rape;
See the cameras zooming in, for everyone to gape.
"How are you feeling, Mrs. Blank?" Don't you wonder why
Poor Mrs. Blank is being so reluctant to reply?

That's the stuff for little ones – what! You're never crying!
Blubbing like a baby at the sight of someone dying?
In that case you can go to bed, and pretty quietly too!
You may not want to watch this stuff but Dad and Mummy do.

Now it's Christmas – people singing carols in the snow;
Mary, Joseph, Jesus, and shepherds all in a row.
Thank God that's only once a year, and now we can get off it.
If there was nothing but 'Peace on Earth', who would make a
                                                              profit?

Margaret Sparshott, London

The next three poems were all published in the journal of the Bank of England, *'The Old Lady of Threadneedle Street'*. *'The Traveller'* is also a fun poem, and *'The Mother'* and *'The Daughter'* are more serious, but I see that they follow the same theme – that it is a mistake to 'lose yourself' in your care for other people. Mrs. Mackenzie does her duty, but takes herself off in her mind and doesn't let her husband dominate her. The mother, on the other hand, has left no space for herself, and so has nowhere to go when she loses her family; the daughter doesn't thank her for it.

THE TRAVELLER

Mrs. MacKenzie's rooms are neat,
Yet with three sons, a lodger, spouse,
She struggles to defeat defeat
And sweep the chaos from her house.

From seven p.m. her brain is still –
Blank eyed, she turns from stove to sink
And by no effort of her will
Runs bath, darns sock, heats evening drink.

Meanwhile her spouse portentous sits
Upon the sofa, holding court.
He talks of wars, and atom splits,
The place of God in modern thought.

Above the talk, her mind revolves
And speeds beyond the commonplace;
Behind a vacant smile she solves
The problem of eternal space.

So, while her husband ums and ahs
And governments go from bad to worse,
Mrs. MacKenzie, striding stars,
Travels about the universe.

Margaret Sparshott:
First published in 'The Old Lady',
Journal of the Bank of England, 1967

THE MOTHER

This house in which I have lived twenty years,
Woman and girl, as they say,
Has lately become my prison.
Maybe it was one all along
Only I lived so closely
That I thought myself protected
By barriers.
Now they are all dead or gone.

What can I do?
I have forgotten how to live
If I ever knew.
What seemed to me a full life
Was one merely
Inhabited by others.
Nowhere do I find myself
Even if I know what I am.

As a person, I ceased
Many years ago, when I came
Happy to this house
Meaning (the biggest futility of all)
'To devote my life to others.'
I did that alright;
So much so, that now,
My husband dead and children gone,
I remain, like an unquiet ghost
Rootless, yet unable to make any kind of escape.

The house doesn't know me
Because I am not.
The children don't know me

Because I have never been.
What frightens me most
Is that if I were to take those tablets from the bathroom shelf
And die tonight as I could wish,
Nothing would be changed, nothing –
Alive I am not less dead.

So I shan't bother to kill myself
One state of non-existence
Being very like another.

Margaret Sparshott:
First printed in 'The Old Lady', journal of the Bank of
England 1968: *This and the following poem were awarded first*
prize in the New Writers' Competition for 1967.

THE DAUGHTER

Now that I, who left that house
Many years ago
To live more easily away from them,
Have finally married
And moved to another town,
I can hardly remember
The face of my mother.
Father is clearer to me
Ten years dead, and long disregarded
In the making of decisions.

Do I miss her?
Impossible to say.
Certainly I have no need of her.
Husband, home, work,
No children,

Fill my life sufficiently.
Sometimes I see the others,
Except my youngest sister
Who went to Australia
Before Father died.
Sometimes also I feel guilty about Mother,
Who gave me the best years of her life, I suppose,
But not often
And not for long.

She should be happy enough
Shouldn't she?
After all, she is free now
To lead her own life
And do all the things she never had a chance to do –
Whatever they may be.

Margaret Sparshott:
First printed in 'The Old Lady',
journal of the Bank of England, 1968

I have always loved London, but I missed the fresh air and quiet of the countryside and whenever I was working in the city I would try to recapture these things by visiting some favourite places. Many times, winter and summer, I would walk along the embankment and across Westminster Bridge, or I would go to nearby Regent's Park and wander into Queen Mary's Garden, lovely in the time of roses, secretive and slightly sinister in winter. The poems *'Eros',* and *'Reflections on the Thames',* were inspired by two of these walks.

EROS

The fitful wind of late November
Drifts the leaves
Down from uneasy branches.
Above the lawn
Battered roses bend,
Sad memories of summer,
From the dry and rustling bush;
Dead garden, where all paths lead
To the silent fountain.
Only at night it dreaming plays
To the restless air,
Scattering a benediction
On weeds floating in rank water.

I stand looking up.
The statue looks down
Out of wet metal, purple, green,
Bronze and black.
Muted shadows play
Over the cold countenance
Giving it fleeting life.
A beautiful, inhuman face –
But as I stand
I see from the parted lips
And down-stretched finger-tips
A soft spray break
Like a chill winter baptism
From the still, metallic heart.
The god looks down –
Down falls the spray,
And I am drenched, doomed,
Drowned in the spring of Love.

So, at the year's end
It was meant
That I should be blown
By the fitful wind
To the empty garden,
The solitary god.
My hands reach up
To touch that slick
Metallic cheek,
Cold and without flesh to my flesh –
Eros, Eros!

Margaret Sparshott

REFLECTIONS ON THE THAMES

Earth has not anything to show more foul
Than this thick river.
Underneath the bridge it passes
Where I stand for a moment to look down
Over cold stone into wet dark.
Deep in memory the water is,
Sucking into its icy torrent
Filth and wreckage from upstream factories.
Those pillars conceal
A thousand miseries;
The bundled rags and newspapers,
The coughing breath
Of old men, destitute but clinging
To the meanest shred of life.
Beautiful in its way, though,

Brown with a slick of oil.
The eddies about the arches
Draw the eyes down, down –
Where I have half a mind to follow.
The bridge voids many, so they say;
They cast themselves ridiculously forth
Upon the bosom of a dubious eternity.

I could stand spinning words all night,
Watching the clever lights
Flicker across the disturbed surface –
A bright flotilla of leaves
Floats quickly past.

What sickly shape is that
Seen through the water?
Oh, smooth slick river
Guard your secrets well!
I do not wish to know them.

Margaret Sparshott

PART III:

GREECE AND CYPRUS

Translations of Greek Poetry and Folksong

In 1967 I left the Bank of England and went to work as a nurse in Greece. This may seem a bizarre thing to do, but I had begun to feel uneasy at the Bank of England. I enjoyed my work there and loved the sense of freedom life outside hospital gave me, but it did not seem a likely place to spend the rest of ones life. As it happens, this move was to transform my life and give it a totally new direction, the effects of which I feel to this day.

Reading the Greek novels of Mary Renault and Mary Stewart, so very different in style and context, led to a great desire to see Greece for myself, and after two holidays spent in Athens and the islands of the Aegean I decided I wanted more. The best way to see and understand the world is to live in it, so I took a post as a nurse in the Aghia Sophia Children's Hospital on the outskirts of Athens, and rented an apartment in the suburb of Goudi. Because at that time I spoke only a few words of Greek I was put to work in the Premature Baby Unit, where the patients did not speak Greek (or indeed any recognisable language), and where there was an English speaking Greek nurse, Penelope.

To my surprise, because my only experience of babies had been in midwifery training, I got on well with the patients. This was, in fact, the beginning of a life-long love of babies that has led me to study their behaviour, try to understand the anxieties of their parents, and subsequently to write and lecture on the environmental problems of the newborn in hospital in an attempt to alleviate the constant bombardment of intrusive and painful experiences they have to endure.

The work shifts at Aghia Sophia were long and the work was arduous and stressful. Nonetheless, I managed to travel around Greece on my days off and holidays. I made many friends, and learnt to speak Greek well enough to be able to converse, and to understand the poems and sing the folk songs popular at that time. Many of these were old, dating back to the time of the Turkish occupation, and I found them so beautiful and interesting that I translated a good many of them; these are the ones found in this section. The folk poems were intended to be sung and had a very distinctive rhythm, which I have tried to preserve.

THE TRANSLATIONS

I am grateful to that excellent anthology, the Penguin Book of Greek Verse, for the Greek and English versions of some of these poems, although I have Greek copies of the poems of Sikelianos, Polemis, and the folk-songs, and the translations are my own. Greek poetry is difficult to translate, because the flowery language, which looks and sounds so well in Greek, seems over purple in English.

The first poem *'Power and Right'* could be relevant today.

POWER AND RIGHT

Listen, kings, who yourselves are wise,
I will now tell you a tale.
A hawk had seized the soft-breasted nightingale
And rose, piercing her with his claws. Hearing her piteous cries

Thus spake he with a harsh voice: "Lady, what is your plea?
I am the strong one; you must do my will;
However sweet your song, you are my kill;
You are my prey, mine to devour or set free."

So said the swift-mounting hawk, rejoicing in his deeds.
"He who slays is mightier than he who sings.
Foolish to fight my power with your weak wings;
You are defeated, shamed – it is your breast that bleeds."

Margaret Sparshott:
translated from Hesiod, 'Works and Days,' (?seventh century)

The next three poems are '*klephtika*'; the klephts were brigands who took to the mountains in the early days of the Turkish occupation, and became freedom fighters. Many of these folksongs date from this time.

SONG OF THE DYING KLEPHT

Mother, if my friends pass by
    Do not tell them I am dead,
And if our kinsfolk should pass by
    Do not tell them I am dead;
That their hearts be not made heavy
    Do not tell them I am dead.

But set a table for their weapons
    With a white cloth spread.
Prepare a bed for them to sleep on
    With a white cloth spread.
When they waken in the morning
    And arise from the bed
And leaving, turn to give you greeting,
    Then - tell them I am dead.

Margaret Sparshott:
translation of a Cretan folk song.

DEATH - A Greek Folk Song

Why are the mountains veiled in cloud, why do they fight the
                                                                wind?
Why do they hide their peaks in mist, are they warring with the
                                                                rain?
It is not the wind that fights with them, nor do they war with
                                                                the rain
But it is Death who shadows them; dragging the old behind
And driving the young before him, he forays across the plain.
He is riding a haggard stallion, and on his saddle bow
He perches all the tender little children in a row.
The old people plead with him, the young kneel at his feet
And clasping their hands the little ones most piteously entreat,
"Death, stop at our village, let's sit by the limpid spring
So that the old may quench their thirst, the young ones play in
                                                                a ring,
And all the little children may weave flowers in a chain."
"But if I stop at the fountain, all those you love will gather
And mothers coming for water will find their children again;
Husbands and wives are sure to meet and cling together again
And all my powers will never suffice to part them from each
                                                                other."

Margaret Sparshott:
translation from the Greek, 18th – 19th Century

'The Eagle' is a metaphorical song, describing the hard winters spent in the mountains by freedom fighters. I love this song, and wish I could sing it for you!

THE EAGLE

To the high mountain, wet and cold,
The eagle flies – the eagle flies,
And there he sits on lonely crag
And shrill he cries – and shrill he cries.
He grips the rock with frozen claws,
And he implores - and he implores
With piteous cry the sun to rise –
"Come, Sun, arise! Come, Sun, arise!
Shine, Sun, the snow and ice to thaw
From feather and claw – from feather and claw!"
Cold and alone the poor bird cries,
"Come, Sun, arise! Come, Sun, arise!"

Margaret Sparshott:
translation of Cretan folk song

There are many later poems written about this black period in Greek history, too. One of these is 'The Hidden School', which tells how the Greek Orthodox Church survived during the Ottoman Empire.

THE HIDDEN SCHOOL

Outside, black mourning veils of hopelessness –
Darkness of bitter slavery grips the hands.
Inside the vaulted edifice of the church,
The church which every evening seems to take
The aspect of a school,
The feeble, flickering candles shed their glow
Stirring up dreams to rouse the sons of slaves
Who gather in their numbers there within.

There in that place, then, dwells the oppressed
Community of slaves, weighed down and bound with chains.
And with hoarse voice the priest, the teacher there
Supports, encourages exhausted hope
With magic words.
There the soul with bitterness comprehends
The agony of her slavery, there she sees
What she has lost, what she yet has, what she must do.

And from the image of Christ in the dome above
Who stops the mouths of the wicked, makes them dumb,
Who throws down into ruin and destroys
And rolls into the abyss the tyrants' thrones;
And from the silence
Which long has blocked the throat of strangled pride;
And from the deathless books of the ancestors
That show the ancient greatness of their past
A deep-voiced hymn is heard to sound
As music coming from another world.
And all the people tremble as they hear
The teacher utter these prophetic words
In voice profound.
'Do not fear darkness! Freedom, like the dawn

In all the brightness of the morning star
To this black night is heralding the day.'
Margaret Sparshott:
                    Translated from I. Polemis (1862-1925)

The charming poem *'The Last Fairy Tale'* needs no
introduction, except to say that as in many international folk
tales the 'bogey man' was used to frighten children into good
behaviour!

THE LAST FAIRY TALE

One by one they took the path,
The princesses and ladies fair.
Upon their horses gallant knights,
And kings from far off lands were there.

Who knows what song they sang to her
As round my grandmother's bedside
They passed between the candle flames
That flickering softly leapt and died.

No-one for love of my poor old Gran
Would kill the Dragon or Bogeyman
Water of life to bring!
Yet my mother kneeling by the bed –
Once upon a time – heard overhead
The beat of an angel's wing.

                    Margaret Sparshott:
                    translated from Lambros Porphyras (1879-1932)

'Easter at St. Luke's Monastery' is said to be an event witnessed by the poet himself. Christmas is a good time to be in Great Britain, but for me there is nothing as exciting as Easter in Greece. Greeks take their religion seriously.

Most people fast during the three days between Good Friday and Easter Day, some indeed for the whole of Lent. On Good Friday the Greeks mourn, and on Saturday the epitaph with the body of crucified Jesus is carried through the streets, strewn with flowers, and people follow weeping – just as is described in the poem by Sikelianos which I have translated. Then at midnight everyone goes to church, very often so many that there is no room for all within, and at midnight the High Priest cries out 'Christos anesti!' (Christ is risen) and the people cry out 'Alithos anesti' (truly risen). Then the High Priest lights a candle from the Pascal candle, lights the candles of the other priests, and so the light goes on through the whole congregation. Then everyone goes home, each carefully nurturing his candle, and on the threshold of their homes they make a sign of the cross in smoke on the lintel. Then the family feast on soup made from the intestines of the lamb they will be eating next day – and on Easter Day there is a great partying and feasting and roasting of lambs on spits, dancing and singing and rejoicing which go on all day long

The ritual for Good Friday is a curious mixture of Christianity and myth. The epitaph is prepared, usually with an image of Christ, and is carried in procession round the streets. The crowds cover the epitaph with flowers as it passes, often with red flowers to commemorate the blood of Jesus, shed for us on Good Friday. But red anemones can also represent the blood of Adonis, a beautiful young man of mythology who was torn to pieces by his own hounds.

EASTER AT ST. LUKE'S MONASTERY.

Of all the women of Steiri
Who had gathered at the Monastery of St. Luke
To adorn the epitaph,
And of all the people mourning there
Who had waited without sleeping
For the dawn of Saturday to break,
Was there one of them, I wonder,
Who remembered that beneath the flowers
And worn enamel of the dead Adonis
Was ever-suffering flesh?
Because pain amongst the roses,
The gentle lamentations,
The soft breath of spring that wafted through the door
Carried their thoughts already
To the wonder of the Resurrection.
Thus, in the wounds of Christ on hands and feet
Buried deep in the sweet-scented flowers,
They saw only
The scarlet of anemones.

But in the night of this same Saturday,
At the hour when from the sanctuary
One candle lights another, and another, all,
And from the step
A wave of light sweeps to the outer door,
They shuddered as they heard
Clear above the joyous shouts
Of "Christ is risen!"
One voice louder than all the rest cry
"Kyria George! Vangelis!"
The hero of the village, there, Vangelis!
The shining light of all the girls, Vangelis!

Whom everyone had considered dead
In the war, long since –
Yet there, with a wooden leg, he stood
Erect at the church door,
And would not cross the step.
With candles in their hands, they stared -
Stared at the brave young dancer,
Whose leaping had shaken the threshing floors of Steiri!
Stared at his face, and at his leg
Which seemed as though nailed to the threshold,
And would not pass.

And then –
I saw it, I who write these simple lines –
From where I stood I saw his mother,
Ripping the coarse black kerchief from her head,
Stoop and embrace that leg,
The wooden leg of the soldier.
And – even as I tell it in these lines –
From the bottom of her heart she cried
"Light of my eyes – Vangelis!"

Even so it was – and after her
All who had gathered there
From the evening of Thursday, crooning, lamenting,
On fire to grieve for dead Adonis, hidden beneath the
flowers,
Now they burst forth together in an unforgettable
Shriek of terror!
And as I gripped the wooden bench
My eyes were blinded with tears.

Margaret Sparshott:
translated from Angelos Sikelianos, 1884 – 1951

The poem 'Skinny-dipping at Vouliagmeni' was written quite recently, and it celebrates a very happy memory; there are few things more ravishing than the feel of warm seawater on bare skin.

SKINNY-DIPPING AT VOULIAGMENI

On a starlit night the four of us
Crammed into the car, and drove to Vouliagmeni.
Barefoot we felt our way down the path,
Where the trees threw spidery shadows,
Stubbing our toes on the slippery stones,
Then out onto the sand we ran
Down to the summer sea.
It didn't take us long to shed our clothes,
And then – I don't remember who was first –
We gave our bodies to the sea, deeper and deeper,
Uttering small screams as the water crept up and up.
Oh but it was not cold, there at the end of summer;
It was like being encased in silk, so tender,
So slippery erotic, so beguiling!
We swam up and down with the waves,
And male and female flesh shone silvery soft,
Marble statues coming to life
In the warm Aegean.
And all the time the stars looked on
As though it was the most natural thing in the world to see,
Four naked middle-aged bodies glimmering in the waves –
And I suppose it was!

Margaret Sparshott, March 2004
First Published in 'Sights to Behold' Forward Press 2007

CYPRUS

The last poem was written after nine months spent in Cyprus working for the International Red Cross during the Turkish Invasion. I worked first for the Cypriot Red Cross, living in the refugee camp of Omidia and working in the Tracing Agency, set up to reunite families who had become separated when refugees fled their homes. Later, because I could speak Greek and could therefore interpret for both Cypriot Greeks and Turks, I joined the ICRC medical teams as a 'flying nurse', visiting those left in 'surrounded' villages in both the North and South who needed medical care but had been unable to escape during the invasion. Sometimes I would supervise the transfer across the Green Line, in both directions, of the elderly, sick and pregnant who needed special medical care; and sometimes I investigated reports which had come through the Tracing Agency of torture and disappearance amongst the Greeks isolated in the North. The poem *'Cyprus, 1974'* tells of this time.

Every incident in the poem is true. Verses two and three describe the conditions of elderly Greeks living in the North and Turks living in the South, who found themselves surrounded by hostile forces. Some of these we managed to transfer, but many would rather stay in their villages, in fear, than travel to an unknown place – and possibly they were right; once they moved from their homes, they were unlikely ever to see them again.

Verse four refers to an abandoned village on the Greek side of the Green Line. It had been a mixed village of Cypriot Greeks and Turks, but the villagers had fled – or so we thought. It was dusk, and we had stopped in the main square, when suddenly a child appeared at the car window, begging for food. We followed him to a big double gate in a high wall. Within, a whole family was living by gleaning from the empty houses and fields. They asked us to give them food, but all we had were stark army rations, when what they needed was sustenance - bread, meat and milk.

Conditions of transfer across the Green Line are described in verse five. When Cypriot Greeks and Turks were transferred, they were allowed to take with them only one suitcase; many of them wrapped all the belongings they could in sheets and tied them into enormous bundles, and these were permitted provided there was only one. Verse six speaks for itself; it is certainly true that a lot of people did very well from the invasion, and not only the Turkish army. Such is war.

CYPRUS 1975

Now rain falls
On the island of Aphrodite.
The peacock sea
Which gently strokes the rocks
Where she was born
Tosses a dirty grey
As muddy torrents make their way
Down river beds choked with dry thorn
And fallen blocks
From ravine walls.

Old men sit
In the cold café.
Broken windows cannot stay
The chill wind blowing from the sea.
Dull-eyed, they watch the sleek cars pass –
They know there's nothing left to loot,
A handful of rags, an old boot,
In a scatter of broken glass.
They wait for whatever will be
The end of it.

Old women weep
And tremble here
Frozen in fear.
Not for them sun-warmed old-age calm;
Their children gone
They know not where,
Their houses and their orchards bare,
They still live on
Enduring threats to do them harm,
Shots that disturb their sleep.

Cyprus 1975   MMS 2007

Lean dogs roam
The empty town –
Dust settles down.
Sunbeams through shattered windows only find
Papers and rags.
But in the street
Is that the sound of hurrying feet,
The grind of bolts on a door that sags?
Is someone left behind
Clinging to a derelict home?

Are they to blame,
Those who must pay
Either because they wish to stay
Where they were born,
Or yearn to quit the place?
What promise or threat
Can make bewildered people sweat
To pack a lifetime in a battered case?
Each man becomes a pawn
Of those who understand the game.

To turn this island into a living hell
Was a good plan
For soldier and for business man;
Both stand to gain,
The one grows rich, the other powerful.
No more
The savagery of war,
Corruption of the peace destroys them all.
Is there a future here beyond terror and pain?
When there is nothing left to sell.

Margaret Sparshott, Cyprus 1975

PART IV:

GENEVA AND PLYMOUTH

Innocent Suffering

Innocent Suffering

Looking back over the years, it is strange how my life has followed a pattern, each thread seeming to lead on almost seamlessly to the next. I can see that it is here in Switzerland that my wandering life style comes to an end, though I didn't know it at the time. At the time, I thought I would go to Switzerland just for three years and then move on – but that was not to happen.

I worked for six years as a Staff Nurse on the neonatal unit of the Cantonal Hospital of Geneva and it was at this time that I first became interested in the effects pain might have on the newborn baby. Up to this time, it was generally believed that babies could not feel pain, and that the reactions they made to pain sensation were just 'reflex actions'. This belief was persistently maintained by many paediatricians in spite of the fact that research was beginning to show that babies could indeed feel pain and had many ways of showing it. There were things that could be done to mitigate this pain, and later I was to write a book on the subject; but this was not until I returned to England. The poems *'First Memory'* and *'The Vigil'* were both written during these years.

After six years at the Cantonal Hospital, I applied for the post of Assistant Director of Nursing at a private hospital on the outskirts of Geneva. This hospital had a large medical staff of Swiss doctors, and a nursing and ancillary staff comprising thirty-two nationalities, whose only common denominator was the requirement to speak French. You might think that this would prove abrasive, but in fact certainly among the nurses this did not prove to be so. Nurses, I have discovered, are universally recognisable – a nurse is identifiably a nurse wherever she comes from, and whatever language of origin she speaks. We all understood each other very well.

One of my duties was to liaise with all English speaking patients and their families in the hospital, of which there were many. It was at this time that I began to study how patients and relatives could be helped to cope with illness and death in a foreign land, away from their homes and friends. I also at this time became interested in various social problems that inspired me to write about people whose experiences were way beyond anything I could imagine. The poems *'Paralysis'* and *'Ibrahim'* are about people I met in this hospital.

I returned to England in 1986, and worked as a staff nurse on the Neonatal Intensive Care Unit in Derriford Hospital, Plymouth; back to my old profession of caring for babies. Here, my interest in pain and the environmental problems of the newborn in hospital became a practical study in how nurses were to understand the language of babies, and this was the time when I began to write about the things I had observed and learnt over the years, and to illustrate my writing by pencil drawings.

Babies can't speak, but the language they use, of cry, of grimace, of body movement, can be read and used in caring for individual babies in individual ways – a 'matter of identity' indeed. Life for newborn babies in intensive care is solitary and painful, but there are ways to make this life easier, by the avoidance of inflicting painful procedures without analgesia, by methods of comforting and consoling sick babies, by creating a world of light and darkness, music and silence, warmth and security, and above all by including both parents in providing this world.

After writing several articles on infant behaviour, and the effects of pain and environmental pressure on a new baby, particularly one who is sick or premature, all these things were put together in the book *'Pain, Distress and the Newborn Baby'*, which was published in 1997 and met with some success; the poem *'First Memory'* was published in this book. I also began to lecture in England and abroad, thus making many friends amongst nurses and doctors from Europe, Canada and America, all concerned with the study of pain.

Later, I became interested in the life and rights of the foetus, and wrote articles and lectured on the subject. I also became interested in the bereavement of parents losing a baby before, during, or soon after birth. This is a special grief, as the parents lose not only a loved and wanted child, but also that child's future. What were those months of waiting and expecting, and, yes, discomfort, for? Most of the poems in this next section are concerned with babies before and after birth, and how difficult it is to make sense of what is happening to them, for both parents and caregivers.

POEMS

I wrote the poem *'First Memory'* while I was working on the Neonatal Unit at the Cantonal Hospital.

This was the first time I had really registered how very much babies subjected to 'intensive care' suffer pain, from the ventilators which keep them breathing, from the intravenous fluids which keep them nourished, from the frequent blood tests which check their progress, and from the injections which treat infection; in Athens, all antibiotics had to be given intramuscularly, and legs and arms became as stiff and hard as pieces of wood.

The particular baby in this poem had been subjected to so many injections and insertions of needles that his scalp and body were a mass of scars. He had a septicaemia which nearly killed him, but in time he did recover, only to remain curiously distant from his caregivers. He appeared lethargic, slow moving, as if each part of his body had to be protected, and he avoided eye contact. It was worrying. He had the knowing look of a mistrustful old man. Later, I recognised this behaviour in other babies subjected to long periods of painful procedures; it is as though any resistance has proved useless, so why try?

'Containment' is a method of gently holding a fragile baby, when it would be too dangerous to stimulate him by stroking him. The drawing shows this hold.

FIRST MEMORY

I remember.
I remember yes
That blissful floating
Warmth, ease,
Darkness deeply coloured.
Muffled sound,
Muffled sound.

Until I am wrenched forth
The bones of my head moulded together –
Agonising compression –
Tearing, forcing,
A sharp slap, and the first
Painful breath,
Bitter light without colour
And cold.
I remember the cold.

I cry, eat, sleep,
My knowledge is
A warm bed,
Arms that enfold;
Soft voices soothe, beguile –
I remember security.

Breathing tires –
Your hands demand.
Breathing pains –
Your hands command
My limbs and body, bear them down.
Hands with needles probe my spine.
Hands with needles pierce my veins –

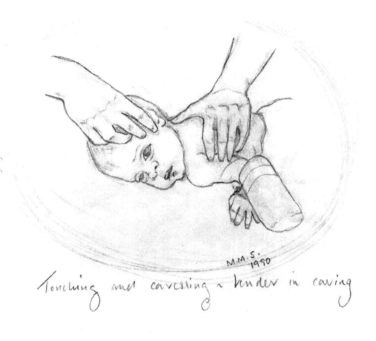

Touching and caressing - tender in caring

M.M.S.
1990

Containment
Touching and caressing
- tender in caring

Helpless I scream into your face
Whose lines I have not learned to read;
Helpless I struggle to be freed
From hands gripping like a vice.

Now your hands are tender and kind –
Those ruthless hands that kept me pinned –
But I have learned to recognise
The hard and forceful hands that bruise
Beneath the soft hands that caress.
 I feel your hands –
I remember the pain.

I look at you with the eyes
Of a wise old man;
My eyes accuse.
Could they speak
They would demand to know
Why you torment me so
Then kiss my cheek –
But memory will remain.

Memory lies deep
Where thought and knowledge sleep.

Margaret Sparshott, Geneva 1979.
First printed in: Pain, Distress and the Newborn Baby,
by Margaret Sparshott, Blackwell Science, 1997

The poem 'The Vigil' is based on a mother whose little girl had an untreatable heart condition. At the time, she was a beautiful, apparently perfect baby, rosy and well, but the mother knew this would not last. Sadly, she blamed herself for her child's illness; her first child was aborted because he was conceived while she was obtaining a divorce from her first husband. This was the child of her second husband; the mother thought she was being punished for the abortion, and nothing we could say would shake this belief.

MMS 2002

"I will not forget you . . .
I have held you in the palm of my hand"

VIGIL

Almighty and most merciful Father,
Why have you played this cruel trick on me?
Nine heavy months of patience mocked
By days of aching vigil at the side
Of my dying child.
For what crime
Do I deserve this hideous punishment?
Have you no miracle for me?
How quietly she lies.
There is no suffering for her now,
Though suffering must come, surely,
At the last moment.
They say there is no hope of life;
So I sit here
Watching her sleeping face,
Waiting for that rosy hue
To blacken in the last great failure.
I weep –
My eyes are sodden with weeping;
I dare not close them now,
I am fixed here
With stretched and burning lids
To the last breath.
Almighty God,
Show me your power –
Most merciful Father,
Where is your pity?

Margaret Sparshott, Geneva, 1980

The next three poems were written after I had moved from the Cantonal Hospital to Hôpital de la Tour, where I was the Assistant Director of Nursing. One of my duties was to visit every department of the hospital each morning, to see if there were problems and to listen to complaints. This way, I came to know many of the patients, and was able to offer practical help to those from overseas, particularly those who spoke only English.

The drawing of 'Ibrahim' is not a portrait – it is a composite picture, taken from photographs, and I drew it from memory, but it is very like the way he looked. Ibrahim was a patient on a ward where the Head Nurse was from Tunisia, and so could speak his language, which is how I come to know a little about his life. We were all deeply sorry for him; there was no one from his family with him to help or give comfort, and all he longed to do was to go home.

Ibrahim

IBRAHIM

He had no watch;
His ram's bell woke him
At daybreak, and rang
Him down to sleep at night.
He was a lord, a king,
Master of the desert, rich and proud,
With daughters who would serve him
And sons to obey his will.

Now here he sits
In the Swiss hospital.
He will not lie on the bed,
Instead he chooses
The corner of the room
Facing the window,
With only the prayer mat to keep him
From the bare floor,
And only when he prays.

His skin is a running sore.
Humiliated and in pain,
Watched over by women
Not of his race
Who tend, but do not serve,
This corner of the room must be his throne;
His prayer is shared with infidels.
Foreign, female hands anoint his loins
With unholy, stinking grease.

When all was done that could be done,
The skin improved, the cancer
Still alive and well,
With tears he pleaded for his home,
That Allah would be merciful.
But mercy was not on the list
Of medication, so
It was planned that he should go
To yet another alien place;
Where he would plead in hopeless prayer
For healing that was not the goal –
The only purpose was to spare
The healers from that failure, Death.
His fate decreed it was his time to die.

.

Who could grieve?
Yet I believe
It was a cruel thing we did
To Ibrahim, who died alone
With infidels on foreign soil,
With no ram's bell to ring him up to heaven.

Margaret Sparshott, Geneva 1986

Paralysis' is about a man who was flown to the hospital from North Africa; he had suffered a massive stroke. His wife, who had never left her country before, was flown over to be with him. He was completely paralysed, but after a time it seemed he could communicate by blinking in answer to questions – nothing more.

Eventually he was repatriated. I never heard from them again, so do not know what happened to him. Probably his wife could not bear to think of her stay in Switzerland.

PARALYSIS

Out of the darkness
He hears strange voices speaking,
Sees familiar faces mouthing;
Mute, he strains towards them –
He cannot speak.

A hand stretched out –
He is there to take it
Only in the fullness of his teeming brain,
Bursting to bear fruit;
But the tree is dead that bears it.

And how is he to live with that?
A listener and receiver only
Of legions of indignities,
His body a machine with batteries
Never more to be fired.

Never to move again!
So, since he cannot command his hand
He sets his will to dying;
Living hand may be too weak –
But will is strong for death.

Margaret Sparshott, Geneva 1985

One New Year's Eve, at the same hour, at midnight, an old man died in our hospital and a baby was born – so, *'Christmas and Easter'*!

CHRISTMAS AND EASTER

This is the time of music and song;
   Christmas is here!
This is the time for bells to ring out
   The dying year.

The music is My music,
   The song My song.
Mine is the change that peals for you
   Life-long.

I laugh with you your joy,
   I weep your pain.
With you I am born, and die,
   And live again.

In your death, there I am;
   In your birth I take My part.
My birth and death turn upon the year
   Within your heart.

All seasons come together now.
   After My birth, the old year dies
To be born again. You mourn My death,
   And I arise!

Death comes to an old man on New Year's Day;
  At the same hour a boy is born.
Tears of joy are shed with the tears
  Of those who mourn.

At this time, with newborn and old,
  Behold Me upon the earth.
Christmas and Easter, birth and death –
  And again, birth.

Margaret Sparshott:
A shorter version of this poem was first published in
'A message of Hope' Triumph House 1998

The next three poems were written after I returned to England to work as a neonatal nurse in Plymouth. To bring myself up to date I took a course in Neonatal Nursing, and chose for my thesis 'Pain experience and the newborn baby' because I was worried by the amount of trauma endured by the babies during their treatment, and the conviction by many (but not all) medical staff that such experience did not exist.

Just as hurtful as the pain endured by babies in hospital is their separation from their parents. Of course it won't help very sick babies to be caressed too much – they need rest – but it is heartbreaking to see parents standing helplessly by the incubator, peering through the Perspex. But there are small acts of care they can perform, such as offering a gentle touch or a finger to hold. *'Separation'* and *'Lament for a Daughter Born Too Soon'* show two sides to this sad time.

Usually, as time goes by, parents abandon their grief for the perfect baby of their dreams, and come to value the small, delicate but incredibly tough individual they really have.

Separation.

SEPARATION

For many a day now I have looked up at this face;
There is a hard substance between
Us two – still it is there in its place –
Half seen.

I cannot tell who it is.
There is nothing to show
That the face has anything to do with me,
Locked here below.

There is no dark, no quiet;
Always, everlasting light.
Only, now I see that the face has gone –
So it is night.

Alone, here I lie
Alone. There is nothing else but pain.
I feel the pain but am too weak to cry;
Perhaps morning will show me your face again.

Is it your hand that holds mine?
I do not know it.
Whatever love there is, from you to me,
You cannot show it.

Only – day after day you are here;
No warm, gentle touch
Save your hand upon mine – today again you are here.
Do you love me so much?

Margaret Sparshott (later than 1989)

LAMENT FOR A DAUGHTER BORN TOO SOON

My baby was born too soon and too small,
A full three months too soon and too small;
She doesn't look like a baby at all
But "She's beautiful", they said.

They told me my baby was beautiful,
"She's beautiful", they said.
Born too small, but "She's beautiful,
She's beautiful", they said.

To me she is not beautiful,
I do not see she is beautiful;
I feel she is not my baby at all –
But I smile and bow my head.

They told me to look on the light side;
"Don't sit in the dark", they said.
They told me to look on the bright side;
"There's always hope", they said.

For me there is no bright side,
For me there is no light side;
I only can see the dark side,
Yet I smile and bow my head.

They said I'd feel better tomorrow;
"Live from day to day", they said.
It will all seem different tomorrow,
"Don't think of tomorrow", they said.

For me there is no tomorrow;
There never will be a tomorrow;
Today has defeated tomorrow –
But I smile and bow my head.

The baby of all my hopes and desires
Is hidden from me by tubes and wires.
She is tied to life by tubes and wires –
And I wish that she was dead.

I cannot tell them the grief I feel;
I dare not tell them the guilt I feel –
I'm afraid to tell them the anger I feel.
So I smile and bow my head.

Margaret Sparshott (later than 1989)

After retirement, I continued to write and lecture on the subject of pain experienced before birth. I do not identify with either the Pro-choice or Pro-Life groups, but you will understand why, for me, after years of caring for them, babies born at and after 24 weeks' gestation have identities, and are beautiful.

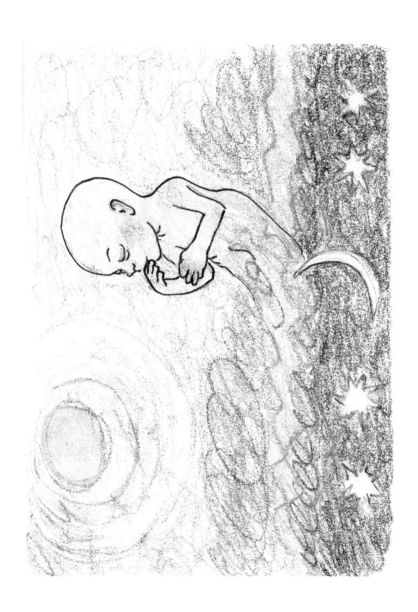

CREATED AND CREATOR

Swimming in darkness is my life.
I taste and smell you, Water of Life;
Before I draw breath
You breathe for me.
A strong cord joins us
And nourishes me.
I can hear your far-off calling.
I can hear the nearby throbbing
That marks the beating
Of another heart than mine.
My heartbeats quicken,
Responding to your joy;
They slow and weaken,
Answering your fear and pain.

Creator, Mother,
Here I float safe and warm.
I wait the time I must become
A child, a person, separate from you.
He who made us both
Knows my unformed body,
Sees me in my tiny parts,
Plans what I am meant to be.
Mother, in my helpless wait,
Respect the creature you have formed –
Without your leave, there is no life.

Without your leave, there is no life.

Margaret Sparshott:
First published in
'A Field of Dreams' Triumph House, 1998

PART V:

GREEN THINGS AND

OTHER MATTERS

GREEN THINGS AND OTHER MATTERS

When I returned to England I bought a small terraced house on the edge of a residential estate in a village on the North West corner of Plymouth, which had the advantage of being both in the town and in the country. I have a garden that runs downhill to a field bordering a creek off the River Tamar. On the other side of the creek, a steep hill of trees rears up to the skyline, and beyond that is nothing but countryside for many miles. In the morning, I can watch the sun creep slowly down the hill; I can see the river mist drift up the valley, and I can watch the gulls fly up and down. All these things I have put into poems.

These next poems are on a variety of subjects. They are not put into chronological order, nor do most of them need any explanation; they express what I feel about the natural world, about love, about music – about a miscellany of things.

POEMS: NATURE RED

It's good to have fun sometimes! These verses and limericks were written for a BBC competition: '*The Shrike*' won a commendation.

ECOLOGICAL NONSENSE

No matter how speedily
  The wildebeest can run
A hungry lion with a bit of a sprint
  Can easily pick out one.
A wildebeest
Is a juicy feast
  For another animal –
  But not a cannibal.

The wonderful news from Brazil
Is that primates may prosper – but still
  The tamarins "great day"
  Could be magicked away
If prospectors move in for the kill.

As we think of our leafy U.K,
"How green are our valleys!" we say.
  But elsewhere the wood
  Will be going for good
If we loot the world's forests this way.

A well-balanced diet, the shrike's;
It keeps a full menu on spikes.
  Without such a larder
  Its life would be harder –
And besides, it can eat when it likes!
Margaret Sparshott 2004

JAGUAR

'Cat man, Makur, the Matis man
Who killed a man-eater,
Harnesses the Jaguar's powers
For his next hunt';
He hunts the cat that eats your soul.

The jaguar is invisible, says the Matis man,
But he feels and smells its presence.
When he hears that rasping cough
It brings him out in gooseflesh
However hot it may be –
The sound of the true wilderness.

And then he sees it, in the undergrowth!
Paws forward, head down,
Eyes staring yellow/green into velvety dark brown -
Rosettes of black on gold, spots before the eyes -
Tracking down his soul.

How to describe this mythical beast,
Caught for once in the open, real at last?
IT IS BEAUTIFUL –
Beautiful.

Margaret Sparshott:
Based on the article: 'A cat in hell's chance'
By Nick Gordon, from: BBC Wildlife, July 1999

GOD KNOWS

Gulls are flying down the valley –
  But can you tell me why
Wings that are white against the trees,
  Are black against the sky?
    What is it makes the eye
See feathers, which are white,
Seem black against the light?

Wet pebbles glistening on a beach
  Are rainbow coloured, each.
Furtively, I pocket some
  And take them home.
When taken from my pocket, they
Emerge a neutral grey.
  But why
This subtle change, from wet to dry?

At half past four
  In the black night, why
Does a pheasant cry
  Once, and no more?
And then, at five,
A fox I hear
Call sharp and clear –
  Is the pheasant still alive
  In the black night, at five?

Don't ask me why;
God knows, not I!
                    Margaret Sparshott

'Tabitha: or nature on the lawn' is in fact one of the most recent poems I have written, but she belongs here.

Tabitha was Elizabeth's cat. I met Elizabeth and her husband John on holiday in Greece, before I went to work there, and we were friends for many years; five of the poems in the last chapter of this book belong to them. Elizabeth died from Altzheimer's disease in December, 2005.

Now Tabitha is John's cat; when she hears him on the stairs in the morning, she rushes to clear her bowl, so that she can greet him with silent mews, pleading for breakfast. This particular day, she had no need of breakfast, and she quite spoiled mine!

TABITHA: OR NATURE ON THE LAWN

A warm July morning,
Sunshine, birdsong,
Breakfast on the lawn –
This must be Paradise!

So here comes Tabitha
Mincing her stout self
Across the grass;
She sits by the rock wall,
And sits,
And sits –
And leaps!

And she brings the foolish mouse
Across the grass,
And she stops six feet from me;
Now she has **her** breakfast!

Crunch,
Crunch,
Crunch **crunch** –
Somehow toast and marmalade
Don't seem so idyllic.

Now she lies upon her back
And shows me her white front,
Whiter than white from the ministrations
Of her pink, abrasive tongue.

Oh beautiful Tabitha!
All the same,
I hope there are no mice or cats
In Paradise –
Unless they are the same size.

Margaret Sparshott:
Green Farm, February 2007

POEMS: NATURE GREEN

This next poem was written during a holiday with my sister on the waterways of Russia. How often does one hear a nightingale these days? But no-one seemed to notice it.

BETWEEN MOSCOW AND ST. PETERSBURG

On the waterways
Between Moscow and St. Petersburg
The slaves built many locks.
Very splendid they are, too.
And once, when the boat was silent and still,
Waiting her turn to pass through;
When golden evening light outshone
The gold and silver birches -
There, more golden even than these,
A nightingale sang among the trees.

Margaret Sparshott 2004

Maybe because of the unsocial hours of nursing, and the frequent periods of Night Duty, I tend to wake at night and feel as though it is day. The only thing to do is to get out of bed, make a drink, read, or, as in this case and weather permitting, take a *'Night Walk.'*

NIGHT WALK

What time is it?
A quarter past three –
No sleep!
Get up, then,
Go downstairs –
Do not turn on the light.
Unlock the back door
And enter the shining garden.
Stand barefoot, but the stones
Seem still warm
In the still, warm night.
Even the wakeful trees
Seem to retain a little green;
Shades of dark, and
Light in the starlight.

So, look up at the stars.
How dispassionate they seem!
How remote they are!
What a privilege to see them,
Layer upon layer as they gleam,
Some seemingly nearer to earth,
Some unbelievably far.

How they shine
With heavenly brightness!
The stars do not love,
Nor do they hate;
They are benign.
They were there, moving across the sky
At the beginning, and at the end
There they still will be –
How far they seem!

They can do without me!
So, leaving the trees and the stars
To be themselves
In the deep of the night,
Barefoot back to the house;
Lock the door,
Climb the stairs
To bed –

And sleep.

Margaret Sparshott August 2006

'Wistman's Wood' is a very strange poem, and I can't remember how I came to write it – it must have meant sense at the time. Perhaps it was a dream! But the real Wistman's Wood on Dartmoor is even stranger. It is one of the oldest oak woods in England; you would think that these gnarled and lichened forms would be incapable of ever showing another leaf, but unfailingly, every Spring, they are covered in young green. So the wood is coloured green and grey; green leaves on green moss, and grey trunks and branches on grey rocks below.

WISTMAN'S WOOD

Should I by grief renew my saint
  To give her life, to give her breath?
  To cause her body to reform –
And shall she die another death?

She died upon this lonely moor,
  Where oaks could shed their leaves for her;
  These fallen leaves became her shroud,
This rocky cave her sepulchre.

She died beneath that rolling sea,
  Her body rocked beneath the wave.
  Valley and stream became a hearse
To bring her to this lonely cave.

They watched her here, in Wistman's wood,
  As from this lichened branch she swung.
  Her feet becalmed on mossy rock,
Between two murderers she hung.

I seek her grave beneath the trees
  All seeing and all knowing they!
  But memories have withered them –
More old than old, they cannot say.

I seek her grave among the stones;
  Their coldness speaks of mortal pain.
  I would recall her from this place
To live a life and die again.

These ancient oak trees crawl the hill;
  The stones long tumbled quietly lie.
  No bird sings, nor no bear pursues –
A place to render and to die.

Margaret Sparshott, 2000

The next two poems are about music, and the third too in a way. I have always loved music, and at school was fortunate in having an eccentric but inspirational music mistress. She had no use for the unmusical child, but she had her 'créme de la créme'. She encouraged me to play the cello, and I played in the school orchestra and quartet and trio. I also sang in the school choir, the church choir, and the Rochester Cathedral Choral Society. Every year, Miss Turner would take us to Benenden for the Summer School of Music, where we rehearsed for a week either in the orchestra or choir, and then gave a performance on the last day. This was a wonderful experience for us growing girls - quite a number of well known musicians went there!

Years of the unsociable hours of nursing, and living abroad, made the practice of music impossible, but as soon as I retired I joined the Plymouth Philharmonic Choir, and renewed the pleasure, remembered from school days, of making music with others.

'The Ballad of the Personal Stereo' was written for a BBC competition, which it didn't win! I wrote it in all sincerity at the time, but since then I have become more aware of the value of personal stereos on journeys. We use rehearsal tapes of the voice parts for choir concerts, and rehearsing on long train or car journeys is wonderfully useful.

The two poems, 'Music' and 'Singing The Dream of Gerontius' come from the special pleasure of making music with other people. They are similar, but 'The Dream of Gerontius' describes a particular concert. It is incredible that one man can inspire and control three choirs and an orchestra, and know precisely what everyone is doing, and when. Everyone is remembered and directed; voices and instruments must play as one. That is the work of the conductor.

POEMS ON A MUSICAL THEME

BALLAD OF THE PERSONAL STEREO

Five men sat on a Southbound train,
  Strangers before that day.
Four men chatted, and chatted again
  To pass the time away.

Four men entered the train alone;
  But each had a tale to tell,
And by the time their journey was done
  Four men knew three men well.

The fifth man sits among them alone –
  The others glance and away –
He twitches and starts, and as if on his own
  He mutters, with nothing to say.

The fifth man hears, but he does not hear;
  He sees but he does not see.
A stereo world is tuned to his ear –
  He is deaf to his company.

Of the five who travelled that day on the train
  Four are departed and gone;
Four who will know each other again –
  The fifth man travels alone.

Alone he travels, alone and lost
  In a world of clatter and clack;
Till the phantom voices, muted at last,
  Let the silence come gently back.
                    Margaret Sparshott, 1999

ON SINGING 'THE DREAM OF GERONTIUS'

Plymouth Philharmonic Choir concert conducted by
Christopher Fletcher
Sunday 2nd April 2006

How can one man -
One brain, two arms, two hands –
Hold in these hands the threads
Of singers, players, all
With their own work to do?
Together, caught in time,
(A time that changes bar by bar)
His two hands hold
The strings of violins,
The reeds of woodwind,
Blast of brass –
Beating of drums –
Soaring of voices high and low,
Fourteen different parts to be blended together
In a tapestry of sound.
In this fashion we are held
To the composer's deepest deep desire;
This music that we make
Is the completion of the Dream,
The conductor's realisation
Of the composer's invention.

This is the conductor's craft.

What we read in this expressive face
Is something deeper than the man himself,
But yet is still the man
Able to hold two hundred souls
And mould them with his hands.

Margaret Sparshott, April 2006

Christopher Fletcher
Director of Music
Plymouth Philharmonic Choir

MUSIC

When music is composed,
Notes fly across the staves,
Wing their way across the measured bars.
This is mathematics that can be heard.

The composer paints the picture, but it is not he
Who brings the notes to life and gives them breath.
This work is done by using other skills;
Instruments, lovingly made by the hands of men,
Sound loud or soft, shrill or deep, acid or mellow,
Obeying the dreams of the composer, the discipline of the
                                                    player,
And the adept hands of the conductor
That move so urgently, so fast –
So lovingly.

The singer then
Takes in breath, watches the beat,
And joins with others in the melded sound,
Obeying the dreams of the composer,
The demands of the musicians,
The harmony of singers, soprano, alto, tenor, bass –
And above all
Obeying too the Master and Director,
As six-armed Jesus blesses the work,
Conducting with his hands.

Margaret Sparshott, February 2004

PART VI:

PLYMOUTH

RETREAT AND ADVANCE

RETREAT AND ADVANCE

I retired from nursing in 1999. Looking back now, I see how much my life up to then has been dominated by work, and travel. The life of a neonatal nurse is rewarding but hard and stressful, and with writing and lecturing there didn't seem much time for anything else. On holiday, I travelled; by bus with a backpack in Greece, with an International English speaking Club in Switzerland, and later, on tours abroad, alone or with my sister.

In all those years I hardly ever went to church. There was an Anglican Church in Athens, but it seemed very elitist and exclusive, attended as it was by visiting business people and embassy staff. I preferred to go to the local Orthodox Church in Goudi. These were long services, sometimes four hours in length, but people came and went as they pleased. The priests followed a strict choral liturgy, but the congregation was very informal, which was good for those of us who worked at the hospital – we could call on the church after or before a shift, and stay as long as we liked.

I have been a member of the congregation of my own local church since retirement, and have written many poems, most of them inspired by an increasing conviction of God's unfailing love. I spend time in Retreat; at Lee Abbey near Lynton, North Devon; Noddfa near Penmaenmawr in North Wales; and the Community of St. Francis in Compton Durville, near South Petherton. Away from home, fed and comfortable, in beautiful surroundings, in good company and, above all, far from the distractions of everyday life, a retreat with periods of silence can wonderfully concentrate the mind, and many poems were written in these wonderful places which are more for

115

advancing than retreating. I remember with gratitude the peace of mind and ease of spirit I have received there.

To attend a Retreat might be more aptly described as an 'Advance'; one retreats from the 'outside world' only to enter an 'inside' world' and can find reassurance and strength to confront the snares, sorrows, and sameness of everyday life.

All these poems are dated, and most of them need no commentary. As you will see, some are written for people, some about people, some are inspired by words heard in talks given during Lent and Advent Retreats, some are written about the drawings, and some of the drawings were inspired by the poems.

POEMS

IN THE GARDEN

'My soul is full of sorrow,
This is my testing day;
Keep watch for me', said Jesus,
'Keep watch for me and pray.

'Simon, are you sleeping?
This is my dying day,
And could you not keep watch for me,
Keep watch for me and pray?'

'Again, I find you sleeping;
You know not what to say.
Your heavy eyes betray your grief –
Keep watch for me, and pray.'

For they could little understand
The meaning of that day;
Nor see, in their bewilderment,
The need to watch and pray.

But we, who know the wondrous tale
That ends on Easter Day –
Who love our dying, living Lord –
Can learn to watch and pray.

Margaret Sparshott, Lee Abbey 1998

'A Morning Walk in January' was written in response to an analysis on feelings, an exercise given to us during a Myers Briggs personality course. I am describing a walk from my home, down across the fields to the creek and back again.

A MORNING WALK IN JANUARY

What do you see?
  My moving boots mounting the slope.
Sleeping gardens, skeleton trees.
Cars moving slowly, gently – no hurry now.
Tamerton Lake glimpsed between roofs.
Then down the hill I go
To the sluggish creek;
Oystercatchers, sandpipers,
A solitary egret wading in mud.
Graceful bare branches frame the wood,
Dark red beech leaves hang on the twig.
Ivy ground-cover with bulbs thrusting through,
And over the creek the steep hanger, sky-reaching –
Steep fields green, with no cattle now;
Solid round hay bales, dangerous –
Not Samuel Palmer's serene sheaves,
Shadowing a harvest moon.
Then up the slippery path,
Mud under foot, sad tufts of grass,
Molehills, dog shit, plastic bottles –
People have been here.
A bearded man, smiling, walks his dogs;
An old couple stroll, stopping to watch
The buzzard circling over Station Road.
So down the steps home
Where the untidy garden waits for Spring;

Daphne, flowering early,
Budding forsythia, heather, babies' tears –
I spy a squirrel thieving nuts,
Stealthy cats, pretending they don't care
For birds on sunflower seeds.

In January, on a winter walk, these are the things I see.

What do you hear?
  Softly humming cars in Milford Lane;
Anxious brakes of a van, cornering too fast.
Window cleaners' idle chat, the squeak of scrapers
Setting the teeth on edge.
The fall of letters in the box.
A man whistles his dogs -
No dog so deaf as one that will not hear.
Through the mud canyons
A streamlet hurries to the creek.
A gull's cry – so common a sound.
Birdsong in the hedges, robin, chaffinch, tit;
Brazen blackbirds out-shouting each other;
Chatter-box magpies, yappy rooks,
Gossiping between meals.
High on the hill I hear
A distant bus reversing,
While nearer home a dog barks on and on,
Defending his master from imaginary foes.

In January, on a winter walk, these are the things I hear.

What do you taste and smell?
  Toothpaste on my tongue,
And cold air tasting of iron.
I smell car exhaust, wet earth,

Creek mud, water, and the marshy smell
Of winter woods, fungus-full.
Then, by the steps to home,
The daphne, full in bloom, intoxicates.

In January, on a winter walk, these are the things I taste and smell.

What do you feel?
  Wind on skin, filtering through hair,
Squelching boots in sticky mud,
Back-ache, and the unaccustomed tug
Of winter muscles.
Chilled hands in pockets, where I find
Warmth, comfort;
And fitting and familiar to fingers,
An apt reminder of all things felt –
A tiny wooden cross.

In January, on a winter walk, these are the things I feel.
                                    Margaret Sparshott, January 1998

TONE VALE HOSPITAL

In the hospital garden, Thomasina walked
With a man who thought he was God.
His delusion did not disturb her;
She could not see for what reason (or lack of it)
His wife had rejected him.
He believed he had created
All things.

That was an unhappy time
And an unhappy place –
So many souls distracted
By suffering; so many despairing prayers
Rising from gaunt-walled rooms.
The man who thought he was God
Could not help the hopeless and the homeless,
The lost and the lonely;
And his wife could only cope with him
When he went home to pay the bills.
Perhaps this confirmed the man in his belief,
For are not all debts paid by God?

It was a long time ago
That the man who thought he was God
Walked in the hospital garden with Thomasina;
Now Thomasina, in the garden of her life
Knows that she walks with God.

Margaret Sparshott, February 1998

The next three poems were written on a silent Retreat at Noddfa, a Roman Catholic convent in North Wales; from the spacious grounds on the slope of a mountain, one can see right across the cold sea to Anglesey.

All manner of people attend these Retreats, Catholic and Protestant; the hard working nuns of my poem were enjoying a rest, but one couldn't stop them from trying to take on themselves all the chores, which we were supposed to share. They were wonderfully skilled at 'keeping silence', since this is how they lived their lives. With gestures, body movements, and facial expressions they made themselves perfectly understood – just like my babies!

THE LITTLE SISTERS OF THE POOR

Opposite me in the chapel
I see the Little Sisters of the Poor;
Their eyes are open
Shining behind their spectacles.
The calm, big-knuckled hands,
Smooth and cool,
Are folded gently in their laps.
They are praying.

When I am old
And am no longer mistress of myself
I would like to be prayed for in a place like this
By the Little Sisters of the Poor.
They would care for me.
They would wake me and wash me
And brush me and comb me
And sit me up smartly in my favourite chair.
They would feed me in no time –
One, two, one, two –
And wipe the egg from my chin.
They would walk me in the garden
And briskly deposit me on my favourite bench;
There I would sit in the morning sun,
Eyeballing the sheep through the roses,
Those guilty trespassers
From neighbouring fields.

Then, when I die,
They would wash me and comb me again for the last time,
And there I would lie, hands folded on breast,
Mourned by the Little Sisters of the Poor.

How good
To be whisked up to Heaven
By the dusters of nuns,
Born on the wings
Of their fluttering prayers!

Margaret Sparshott. Noddfa, August 1998

I could see the squirrels in this next poem from my window; there were many of them, and I was terrified that one would slip and fall – but they never did.

GOD IS A TREE FOR SQUIRRELS

There are apples under the tree,
Small, rosy apples, half eaten.
Somebody has taken small bites out of every one –
The apple tree is full of busy tits,
Sampling and snacking and casting down;
It is their little beaks which are spoiling the apples.
But wait,
The apples are not there for me to admire and taste!
The apples are there for hungry birds
To gain their strength in Autumn.
These cast-off remnants
Will rot into the ground
Ready for renewal –
Renewal of apples for next year's harvest –
Renewal of next year's tits.

If I look up
Through the five-fingered hands of the sycamore,
The shifting layers reveal

Little blue bits of Heaven;
And down through the leaves and branches
Sail the green-veined angel-wings.

The wrinkled oak
Grows untidy leaves.
This is an old tree, and familiar.
Slow, slow it is to show
Green leaf in spring.
Long, long it clings
To worn brown leaves in autumn.
Am I an oak, old, gnarled and stubborn?

Surely this beech
Is for the squirrels!
How they rejoice amongst the topmost boughs!
How they cling and swing
And stretch to catch
The nethermost nuts!
One little hand supports a body
Smooth and lithe
And light as dust.
They feast and fatten for the winter storms.
I catch my breath
To see one squirrel bounce
Upon the leaves –
But no, this is their kingdom,
They were made for this.
Heavy and earthbound
I may look up and marvel;
And, if God permits,
Soar in spirit through the copper leaves.

Margaret Sparshott, Noddfa, August 1998

125

IS GOD A TREE?

Is God a tree?
Is God a cedar
Strong in Lebanon among the fallen columns,
Until the branches are leaf-raped –
Bomb blasted on the battle-field?
Is God a pine
High on a Scottish mountain,
Sheltering beasts and birds of prey?
Does He stand in the graveyard, solemn yew,
Darkly sheltering the silent dead?

God says 'A tree carried me –
But I am not a tree.'

Am I a tree?
Am I a cypress
Loving the hot sun,
Deep roots pillaging the dry earth,
A black silhouette on a terracotta hill
Reaching and stretching
To claw at Heaven?
I would like to be an olive
On a hillside in Delphi,
One amongst many,
Turning my green and silver leaves
In the bright white light of Greece.
Your bread and my olives feed many hungry mouths.

But God says 'You are not a tree –
You nailed me to a tree.'

Margaret Sparshott, Noddfa, August 1998

FLOOD

'O ye Sun and Moon, bless ye the Lord ...
O ye Waters that be above the Firmament, bless ye the Lord ...
O ye Showers and Dew, bless ye the Lord ...
O ye Lightings and Clouds, bless ye the Lord ...
O all ye Beasts and Cattle, bless ye the Lord ...
O ye Birds of the Air, bless ye the Lord ...
O ye Children of Men, bless ye the Lord ...
O ye Stars of Heaven, bless ye the Lord ...'

Sun and Moon sleep.

Mist weaves in spectral shape and form;
Waters above and Waters below spin and drift.
Thunder rolls and mutters, coming in threat,
Menacing near at hand.
Mad claps and yells, laughter of lightning
Applaud a crazy God.

Elements rejoice.

Whales rejoice in wrack and wash:
In Waters below and above they leap and breach,
Great flukes hurling froth and foam.
With skilful feathers, Fowls of the Air
Flirt with fume and spume in freedom,
Flying in flying spray.

Fish and Birds rejoice,
Dancing with the elements.

MMS
May 2004

128

In the chill morning, Ark floats in mist;
Animals snuff the air, uneasy with each other;
Each smells rank scents of blood and terror
Foreknowledge of Death on sea or land.
Restless, they rock the boat.

Nurturing the Beasts
Women kill fear with tenderness.
'Is there enough for all to eat?
Will we starve? Will we freeze?
Will we drown?
Dare we ask God how he has planned our death?'

Noah and his sons peer beneath hands;
See nothing but vapour of Waters above,
Hear nothing but hiss of Waters beneath.
The birds do not return.

Waters rejoice, Whales rejoice –
Sun rejoices.

Sun says, 'Here am I, where I have always been.
I send you God's Bow, God's covenant.
Come, see me suck up the Flood, see the spouts and springs
Of the waterfalls – Water returning to place.'
Animals turn to the forest, Birds to the air,
And new man Noah returns to his home;
Farmers and shepherds develop the land.

Beasts and Cattle and Children of Men rejoice.

Sun sleeps at the dawn of night;
Beyond the Moon, cold stars lean over
To keep chill vigil, blessing the dark;

And God moves on through the Universe,
Creating new worlds as He goes.

'O ye Heavens, bless ye the Lord:
praise him and magnify him for ever.'
Margaret Sparshott, June 1999

The drawing for *'Scale into Skin'* came before the poem. It was drawn for a friend at Lee Abbey in 1998, from a photograph of 'Christ Creating Adam', a statue in the North Portal of Chartres Cathedral.

SCALE INTO SKIN

When God created Adam
He drew him from the mud by his gills;
Saw Man in the fish.
Looking down at the flapping tail
God smiled, and smoothed His hands
Over prickly fin and slithery scale,
Over and over the cold wet flesh.
God smiled, and flexed His hands,
Gave the rib cage a push,
Tugged the lungs out and in,
Kneaded scale into skin.

At last the dazed creature, gasping and blinking,
Climbed up through the welter of salt and spray,
Saw the face of love, the smile of greeting –
Warmed himself in the sun of the new day.
Margaret Sparshott: First published in 'Celebrations'
Anchor Books 2006

Scale into skin

I resurrected *'Profane Love'* whilst sorting my papers and can't remember when I wrote it – so I can't have been so very old! But together with *'Sacred Love'* it seems to show the two sides of ageing, bad and good.

BETWEEN BIRTHING AND DYING - PROFANE LOVE

I never let you guess
That at your touch my heart would leap to flame
And burn the sun from Heaven!
Dear Soul, you'd never understand
In a thousand years, that fire –
You might suppose the funeral pyre,
The embers of that blaze would warm me still –
But now, God knows,
I am grown old and frozen cold,
And the pride I cherished in my guarding hands
Has left me comfortless.
Poor fool, you say?
Death's my companion, like a cat, a stray
That persists and will not go away.
You'ld never understand
In countless years –
Yet weep for me who have no tears.

Margaret Sparshott ?date

BETWEEN BIRTHING AND DYING - SACRED LOVE

It's time to savour winter,
Passion not spent, but fleshless;
To love without demanding
A fleshly satisfaction.
It's time to hear the half-time bell
That sounds the passing of the middle years
Between birthing and dying.
The entry gate is vanishing
Behind the mists of living;
The passing gate is homing,
Austere but not unwelcoming.
There is no longer need to look
Inward to a lonely self;
There's freedom now to gaze abroad
Knowing myself never alone.

The nearer comes that strict approach
The warmer grows that guiding hand -
Not spectral bone, not flesh and blood,
But Being, Loving, Knowing, Thou.

Margaret Sparshott, 2004

We were at Lee Abbey, spending an afternoon, in silence, in Creative Activity (or 'doing our own thing!') I spent more time watching those around me than anything else – and I wrote this poem.

SEARCHING

There are many in this room
Searching for God.
Paint flows on wet paper, hands with pencils draw.
On bended knees, some keep the silence.
Pencils move across paper –
Poems flow like rivers, under
Bridging thoughts.

Who sees God in the Trinity?
Who sees Him in driftwood,
Tumbled flowers,
The fallen leaf of a sycamore?
Who sees Him
In lit candles, shapes and spirals,
Music, falling like a river
Under bridging thoughts?

Mary sees Him in stars,
In the solemn icon of the Virgin of Vladimir –
She sees Him in the river, crossed
By bridging thoughts.

Mary sees God in poems,
And she writes of love and fellowship.

Margaret Sparshott, Lee Abbey, May 1999

'Listen to Me' was written during a 'Quiet Day', spent with other members of my church at the Convent of St. Elizabeth in Plympton St. Maurice.

LISTEN TO ME

"I speak to you in the garden," says the Lord.
"My voice in birdsong, sigh of water, creak of bough.
The Holy Spirit sings in the wind,
Blows through dry leaves.
My garden is the desert", says the Lord,
"I am the midday sun throbbing like a drum;
I stir in soft sand,
Sift through artic snows – wail in the ice-fields.
My voice roars in winter storms, pounds in sea-waves
Beating on rocky shores. The world is my garden.
Listen to my voice in my garden," says the Lord.

"I speak to you in the city," says the Lord,
"My voice cries in the council flat,
Aches in lonely lives,
Cold homes, drab homes, no homes;
Nowhere to go, no-one to hear, no-one to love,
I speak to you, my lost ones
In the city.
Created lives deprived of freedom
Turn cruel and thoughtless,
Drugged by the artifice of virtual reality -
You, the lonely, losers and lost, I speak to you," says the
                                                          Lord.

"I speak to you in the ghetto," says the Lord.
 "You, shut in and surrounded,
Separated from your kind;
Separation not created by me –
Where did you learn these things?
I speak to you – come out into the world.
Those from within who enclose you,
Those from without who fence you in
They do not hear my voice -
But to you I speak, in the ghetto," says the Lord.

"I speak to you in the Church," says the Lord.
"When did I tell you to shut yourselves away?
Come out, come out and answer me yourselves.
Come into my garden, the desert and the ice-fields;
Come out into my city streets, out from my ghetto.
Open your doors, my churches, mosques, and synagogues.
You are all my children – I die for every one."

"I speak to you in the silence," says the Lord,
"Listen to my voice."

Margaret Sparshott, May 2000:
St. Elizabeth's House, Plympton St. Maurice.

ADVENT RETREAT, LEE ABBEY

"I must clear a space for Jesus to be born" –
Hark! Is that the rain?
Oh, now I've lost the thread; I'll have to start again.

I must clear a space for Jesus to be born –
But rats are running; all I hear instead
Are rats' feet running, running round my head.

I must clear a space for Jesus to be born –
But oh! I pray
For Him to come more quickly, chase the rats away.

I must clear a space for Jesus to be born –
He does not need that space, for He
Has all the world to play in; He needs no space in me!

I must clear a space for Jesus to be born –
But no, it is too difficult, too much to ask.
How can He set on me so onerous a task?

I must clear a space for Jesus to be born –
It is not possible! I must be mad
To think He could be housed in one so sick and sad.

I must clear a space for Jesus to be born –
But like the sea
Which ebbs and flows each day, so it is with me.

It's hard to rid myself of tumult, toil and pain;
But still He waits, and I begin again.
I am clearing a space for Jesus to be born.

Margaret Sparshott, Lee Abbey,
November 2002

COME WRETCHED AS YOU ARE
AND LOOK FOR GOD

"Come wretched as you are, and look for God."
I must go seeking Him – but where?
Not in the Church, I have not found Him there.
Could tall and cool cathedral be the place?
Not in quiet cloisters have I seen His face.

"Come wretched as you are, and look for God."
In softly coloured landscape, between walls
Of muted stone, rough-built, His shadow falls;
His shadow only – in that sunlit place
I have not seen His face.

"Come wretched as you are, and look for God."
His Word I've heard and seen
When seeking Him between
The pages of a book.
Surely, this is where to look
For God! But even in that place
I do not see His face.

"Come wretched as you are, and look for God."
In hospital, at midnight, I
Have glimpsed Him with the sleepers where they lie
Helpless in the dark, too weak to cry;
I feel His presence in that lonely place –
I have not seen His face.

"Come wretched as you are, and look for God."
It seems I sense Your presence in every part,
At home, abroad;
Yet I have never found the place
Where I may see Your face.
Where must I look, then, Lord?
"Dear child, you surely know
The word I speak to you is 'come', not 'go!'
Rest now! My face is hidden in your heart."

Margaret Sparshott,
Lee Abbey, November 2002

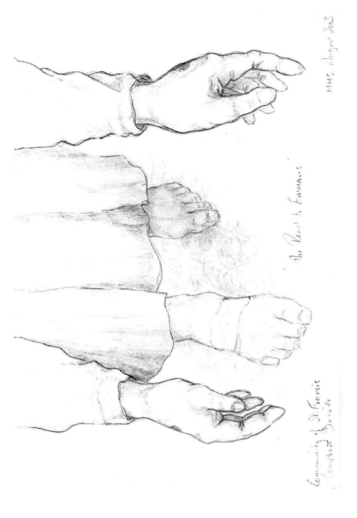

The Road to Emmaus

THE ROAD TO EMMAUS

It occurs to me
They may never have been able to look up
On the road to Emmaus.
Their heavy hearts may have forbidden them
To raise their eyes, and look
At the fair sky.
He who had spoken as the conqueror of Heaven
Had fallen a shamed victim
To a lonely tomb.
Where was His body now?

And so, walking that road
Among the travellers hurrying
To and from Jerusalem,
All they could see were the strong feet
Planted among the stones and dust,
And outstretched, teaching, loving hands.

Margaret Sparshott,
Community of St. Francis, Compton Durville. August 2003

Several of my poems are about solitude. Most of my life I have lived alone, and have become very used to my own company. During the nursing years, I could support hard work and hardship because I could then go home and shut the door on the outside world. I think some people are naturally solitary - and I am one of them.

THE LONELINESS OF THE LONELY

A hover fly catches the only
Small patch of sunlight.
As the leaves move, so moves the hover fly,
Searching, always, for the sun.
In shade the colours dim,
Turning the fly invisible;
But in the sunlight
Colours dazzle, gold and black and brown,
And the blue transparency
Of delicate wings.
Oh what a mystery of happy solitude!

On the bare grass roots
Brown with August,
The settled butterfly
Waits for the clouds to pass.
Nothing moves down there
Save the busy ant hurrying -
Always hurrying away.
But the stillness of the garden, and my own
Stillness
As I stand, leaning on my stick,
Is caught by the butterfly
In one long moment of
Stillness

In hurrying time.
God created time and made it last forever;
Oh what a mystery of stillness
In hurrying time!

And so I think of loneliness,
The loneliness of people;
Not the connected loneliness
Of a hovering hover fly
Or a basking butterfly,
But the aching loneliness
Of those in separation, in longing,
In self-hatred or hatred of those
Around them.
The loneliness of being different,
Of separation by death, illness, pain –
The loneliness of people.
Oh the misery of loneliness!

For the lonely in their pain
There is no God.
The world created by Him
Does not surround them with the comfort
Of its own apartness.
The world is 'on the other side',
Out of reach, out of touch, out of hearing,
Out of sight;
The world is available to everyone and everything,
Except the lonely.
The lonely cannot escape
The prison of their solitude.
Oh the misery of the chains of solitude!

Look in, look in, for it is sure
That God is dwelling in the loneliest heart,
The darkest and most desperate soul,
A well-spring waiting to be tapped.
A man can live in closest company
And still be lonely;
Man and wife, parent and child
Can still be lonely.
It is within, within, the dearest companion
Lives and waits to be called.
And oh, the mystery of that silent, lonely calling!

Margaret Sparshott, Community of St. Francis,
Compton Durville. August, 2003.

There is quite a large community of nuns at Compton Durville. I never knew the name of this nun, whom I could see from my bedroom window, but was impressed by her quiet, contained manner as she sat facing the rising sun.

SISTER NONAME

Sister Noname comes into the garden
As the dawn breaks.
She carries a black bin bag.
She crosses the lawn, takes a chair
And places it with its back to the wall
Facing the East.
She spreads the bag over the seat
Very carefully.
She sits and crosses her ankles,
Carefully placing her sandaled feet.
She crosses her hands

'Sister Noname'
Compton Durville, August 2003
M.M.S.

Sister Noname

Carefully,
Folding them in her lap.
She looks before her; then closes her eyes –
And she is gone.

That quiet nun
Sitting at ease in the garden chair
Is no longer present –
But nor is she far away.
Her presence hovers,
Half in the world
Half heavenward,
Living her other life,
Where no one here can reach her.
Soon she will return, when the bell calls her,
To her quiet self
By the garden wall, in the garden seat
Facing East, into the rising sun -
Sister Noname, whose name is known in Heaven.

Margaret Sparshott,
Community of St. Francis
Compton Durville. August 2003.

During one week at Lee Abbey we were asked to write a psalm, and so I wrote two. The second one was a cry from the heart. I do not find the Christian life easy; it is very hard to let go of responsibilities when the time comes to do so, there is a pride in imagining that no-one can do without you. 'Faith' and 'obedience' are easy words to say, but not so easy to achieve, for me, anyway; they require patience, and work. I include this psalm because I am certain I am not the only person to feel this way; there's comfort in numbers.

LEE ABBEY PSALM - I

Lord, you have created a world of marvellous beauty,
   And have given us the eyes to see it.
Why then do our eyes look on shallow things
   That have no truth in them?
Why do we look for beauty that is false and has no depth?
   Why do we rape the world of its treasures?
Yet you have filled the world with wonderful things,
   And you have given us eyes to see your love for them.
You have shown us how to see, touch, smell and feel, and
                  know what is good.
  We praise you, for the truth of your creation is everlasting
                 and will never be spoilt –
We thank you, Lord. *Amen*

LEE ABBEY PSALM - II

O Lord, you are a hard taskmaster.
  You have asked me to do a difficult thing.
Why me, O Lord? I cannot do it,
  It is too hard for me, I have no strength.
I cry to you, I cry to you and you are silent.
  But in your silence I understand your word:
I must obey, though blind to your purpose –
  I must obey your command, though I do not know your will.

And now, is the work done?
  I only know that I must let it go,
And that is hardest of all.
  It is in your hands, Lord.
I must give back to you this weight you set on me,
  And lift to you my anxious heart for healing.
I may never know how you have used my work
  That is not mine, but done through me by you.
I must not ask for answers, but must try
  To live my life in obedience and trust,
Knowing that I am the tool and you the master craftsman.
  I thank you, Lord, for making me your tool. *Amen*

Margaret Sparshott,
Lee Abbey, February 2004.

I wrote about my father at the beginning of this book; now I must write about my mother.

She was a very strong lady, very proud, very competent. She spent her whole life looking after other people, but unlike 'The Mother' in the Bank of England poem she retained her own identity. People loved and respected her; she was supportive to people who struggled with their lives, and she gave wise advice. She was totally unlike Father in personality; he was laid back and sweet tempered, she was impatient and had temper tantrums which were frightening – but we learnt how to live with them. Mother and Father had been friends from childhood; they had many common interests, enjoyed being together, and obviously loved each other; perhaps their difference in character was a good thing – they balanced each other.

She was a wonderful mother for a child, but was scornful and critical of her adolescent daughters - but then life was not kind to her. She was often unwell, suffered from migraine, and had had disfiguring surgery which deprived her of womanhood (a double mastectomy before I was born, and a hysterectomy during the war). She worked hard, was the unpaid housekeeper when Father was a Housemaster, looking after the little boys as well as her own family, and was moved from pillar to post during the war. Then Father had to retire before he reached pensionable age, and she looked after him until he became too heavy for her; she took the lock off the bathroom door, but she had to drag him out of the bath by his hair while he sat immovable, blue and shivering.

After he became ill, there were no more migraines, and no more tantrums. She would rise to the challenge when she was confronted with trouble; then, she was at her best.

She was not afraid of dying, but she hated being old and incapable; all she could do was 'rage, rage against the dying of the light.'

OUR MOTHER DIED

Our mother was old when she died,
Old and in pain.
We could not have wished her to live
Any longer than her ninety-one years.
She did not wish to die,
But she was angry with her age
And her inability to cook meals,
Organise the house
And boss her daughters.
All that made her strong
Was taken from her by the passing years.
She died early in the morning
In the grey dawn.
She lay in the disordered bed
Ruffled and unkempt,
Her limbs awry
Her hair adrift,
Her staring eyes and open mouth
Seeming to say
'Away, away with you!'
How she would have hated
To be witnessed so unseemly!

So my sister and I
Set about putting it right,
Making it good,
Laying her body to rest.

Open the window, let the winter dawn
Frisk through the bedroom, clean and fresh.
Fetch towels and water,
Soap, sponges and cotton wool;
Wash her tired body,
Straighten the crooked limbs.
Comb the thin grey hair to lie
As it did in childhood,
Soft and fine against her brow.
Close her anxious eyes
And shape her anguished mouth,
Thus to see her lived-in face,
Firm again, firm again,
Noble and stern -
The way she was.

What next?

Take the finest nightgown
From the chest of drawers,
Dress her, cross her hands
Upon her breast;
Bring flowers,
Set them on the bedside table.
Strip the bed, gather the tumbled sheets,
Surround and cover her with fresh linen
Smelling of soap and sunlight.
Draw the coverlet
Up to her waist,
Fold it below
Her folded hands

My mother, Gladwys Winifred Sparshott

Here lies our mother
In her solemn state,
Noble and dignified,
Stern and masterful
And unashamed by death.
Elizabeth and I
Are proud to render her
This last service.

Margaret Sparshott, February, 2004

I drew three pairs of hands for a proposed cover for the book 'Relating to the Relatives: breaking bad news, communications and support' by Thurstan Brewin, of which I wrote a chapter. It was never used, but the drawing made me think of the three people it represents, doctor, relative, and patient, and how different their feelings must be.

THREE PAIRS OF HANDS

These hands are stretched out,
Offering and beckoning.
"Come", they say, "I will give you all I have."
These are the hands of the healer
Who knows he cannot heal;
They ask forgiveness
And they offer hope.
"Trust my hands," says the healer,
"They cannot give you life
But they can ease your death."

Three pairs of hands

These hands are clasped,
Giving each other comfort,
Reassuring each other that they are living and well.
But they are beseeching hands, too –
They beg for mercy, not for themselves
But for the one they love.
In a moment, one hand will stretch to clasp
The cold hands on the bed beside;
Not only do they strive to give,
They grope for comfort for themselves.
How often do the dying need
To comfort the living?

These hands lie gently on the sheet;
There is no stress in them, no anguished clasping,
No sense of a struggle to survive.
These hands have toiled enough; now is the time
For them to be still, for they have
No more work in this world.
They will never grow old.
They will never wither and blotch,
Twist and deform, no,
These hands have abandoned the future,
Accepted the here and now.
There is no more for these hands to do.

Three pairs of hands, enclosing
The very stuff of living –
Consoling, grieving, dying.

Margaret Sparshott, March 2004

HOW TO PRAY

The old lady told the Bishop
She didn't know how to pray;
She said the only way
She knew was to talk to God every day;
But no one seemed to be there.

"So, don't talk to God every day",
 Said the Bishop, "If that is not your way.
Now, listen to what I say –
Perhaps this is how you should pray ..."

So the old lady tidied her room and took up her knitting –
And she sat in her favourite chair;
And the clock continued its ticking,
And the needles continued their clicking
And she gave herself to the peace of the day
And forgot to fret about how to pray -

And suddenly, she was aware
That another Presence was there –
 This was prayer.

Margaret Sparshott, Lee Abbey, March 2005

*Since writing this poem, I have come across the origin of
this story in the book 'School for Prayer', by Metropolitan
Anthony of Sourozh; it actually happened to him. He says: 'and
in the end she said something very beautiful . . . she said "All
of a sudden I perceived that the silence was a presence. At the
heart of the silence there was Him who is all stillness, all
peace, all poise".*

ON EAGLES' WINGS

' ... those who hope in the Lord will renew their strength. They will soar on wings like eagles; they will run and not grow weary, they will walk and not faint. ' Isaiah, 40:31.

Abba, Father,
Anger and rage,
Burn, burn;
Resentment and bitterness
Burn, burn;
Weakness and cowardice
Burn, burn;
Doubt and despondency
Burn, burn.

Abba, Father;
Peace and quietness
Comfort me;
Patience and kindness
Comfort me;
Firmness and courage
Comfort me;
Faith and love
Comfort me.

Abba, Father,
Morning and evening
I rise, I fall and I rise;
In you I trust,
To you I lift up my soul;
Only say the word
And I shall be healed.

Amen.
Margaret Sparshott, Lent Retreat,
Lee Abbey, February 2006

The table in silence

It might seem a contradiction that one should find companionship in silence, but so it is, as *'The Table in Silence'* shows. There was a moment at that meal when everything about us seemed very bright and clear, as though the table and the four people round it were suddenly bathed in light. This took place during a Silent Retreat at the Community of St Francis, Compton Durville. I drew the picture from memory the same evening, and much later, wrote a poem about it.

THE TABLE IN SILENCE

There are four people at this table;
Three of them are before me –
I am the fourth.
The table is spread
With a simple meal,
Bread, cheese, jam and fruit;
Water to drink.

We have been together
Four days now,
And in that time
We have not spoken,
For this is a 'silent retreat'.
We know each other's names,
And we have spoken with eyes,
Brows and hands;
And we have smiled, sometimes laughed,
Because not one of us is skilled
In silence.
It does not seem strange now.

I see these friends,
Companions,
As they sit before me.
I see they are close, but also far away,
Deep in their thoughts and dreams,
Meditating, contemplating,
Alone but not alone.

To me suddenly
Everything is very clear.
There is a brightness on the table,
Set with its plainness and simplicity.
There is a brightness about these three,
And we are all linked, in silence,
By a profound knowledge, too deep for speech.
Words cannot matter
In this communication.

Tomorrow we shall speak
And greet each other,
Surprise each other with places, dates,
Work and play,
Love of books, music, tennis –
Everyday things!

But already we know all we need to know.
Margaret Sparshott, October 2001

The next two poems were written on a Lent Retreat at Lee Abbey. Many people visiting Lee Abbey come from far afield, and after a long journey one of the first things they do when they arrive is to walk up the path to Jenny's Leap. This is a short walk up through the wood to the cliff edge, and from there you can see Lee Bay and the coastline to the West and on a clear day the Welsh coast across the sea to the North-East. If you look down, there is a vertiginous drop to great sharp-finned ridges of rock, running out through restless waves – always restless in that place.

The legend tells us that Jenny's Leap was named after Jennefried, an heiress to the Manor of Lee, who learnt on her wedding day that her unfaithful lover had married another woman. 'Stricken with grief she wandered through the night on the rugged cliffs, and when day dawned, her lifeless body was found at the foot of the precipice under Duty Point'.
(From Lee Abbey: A Brief History)

JENNY'S LEAP

A Lent Retreat in March;
So once again
I climb the path to Jenny's Leap.

Bathed in the brisk sun,
The silver-tipped green grasses
Bend to the will of the wind;
And in the fields below
Sheep graze haphazard,
Turning their backs
On strutting rooks.
Beyond again lies the sea,
Breaking slowly and undulating
After yesterday's storms.
These fields and paths are worn
By happy feet and fleet –
By weary feet and slow.

I have been here at Jenny's Leap
In many moods.
Today I am happy –
But this is a place to be absorbed
By happy hearts and sad.
Sadness cannot turn the colours grey,
Only, it wears a veil
That beauty cannot penetrate.
Suffering knows its place here,
As well as joy and thankfulness.
So many hearts and souls,
Some at war and some in harmony –
Here is a place for all.

It is said
That Jenny leapt for love –
It was not love she found
On rocks beneath the cliffs at Duty Point.
These ledges welcome only
Sure-footed feral goats and gulls
Who leap and plunge for food –
Not love.

Perhaps today
Jenny would not have felt the need
To leap from her high springboard.
Perhaps she would have turned back from the cliff,
To find the Love, so desperately sought,
Already standing at her side.

Margaret Sparshott, Lee Abbey, March 2007

This next poem 'Christ is Risen' was also written during this same Lent Retreat. Like the poem 'Easter at St. Lukes Monastery', it is a reflection of Easter in the Orthodox Church.

I was remembering a programme I saw on Television some years ago. I can't recall the name of the programme or which TV station it came from, but the incident itself I have never forgotten, nor ever will, I think. These may not be the exact words used, but I well remember the excitement, almost rapture, expressed by this unknown man.

CHRIST IS RISEN

'Peristroika' had opened the gates
To Russia;
And the actors went to Moscow to perform
'Uncle Vanya' in English,
To the Muscovites.
There was a full house, but they were perplexed
To know how they had been received;
No boos, no cat-calls certainly,
Some clapping –
But no warmth, no laughter –
Not much to laugh about in 'Uncle Vanya'.

So they were tired and despondent,
Sitting about under the camera's eye,
Not feeling much like talking,
When suddenly, the door swung open
And there, like a rising sun amongst them,
A big and bear-like Russian beamed upon them:
"Welcome, welcome! Ah how splendid!

What an honour to receive you!
What a wonderful day to see
How you in England
Perceive our Russian play!"
The actors stir and smile;
Perhaps the journey was not wasted after all.

But then the smiling man proclaimed,
"Tomorrow it is Easter Day!"
With arms spread wide he greeted them with:
"Christ is risen! Christ is risen!"
Welcomed these souls from happier lands
Where worship would be free.
What could the actors say? What did they say?
Beneath the camera's eye
They seemed completely overwhelmed;
They did not jeer or sneer or lie –
They did not need
To give a smooth reply;
What could you say to "Christ is risen"?

Christ is risen indeed.

Margaret Sparshott, Lee Abbey, March 2007

PART VII:

PLYMOUTH

LAST THINGS

LAST THINGS

The poem 'Elizabeth' was written for a dear friend of many years – kind, intelligent – taken away from us by Alzheimer's disease.

Altzheimer's seems to like intelligent people, and it is sad that the descent into insensibility should be the last thing to remember of both my father, at the beginning of this book, and Elizabeth, at the end. Elizabeth was witty and warm, and had a most beautiful speaking voice, 'ever low, gentle and soft,' like King Lear's daughter Cordelia; the Altzheimer's never corrupted that quality. She was also a skilled musician, and hosted musical evenings of Baroque music, with a group of friends playing old instruments; she played the spinet that was made for her.

Elizabeth died in December 2005, ten months after I wrote this poem, but the music still goes on; the group still regularly meet and play together at Green Farm.

The next four poems recall this friendship.

POEMS

ELIZABETH

Elizabeth is not at home;
You may knock and call to her, but
There will be no reply, not ever.

:

There are recordings of her voice -
That low, gentle, Cordelia voice –
And you would think that:
Look! that is unchanged!
But it is not the same.
This voice, beautiful as ever,
Babbles a rhythmic nonsense,
And if you hear it without listening
You would say
Yes! that is Elizabeth!
But there is no one there.

There was a time, not long ago,
When the uncertain suspicion of wrongness
Made her angry.
Then, that kind and merry face
Puckered in fear and disbelief.
We lied to her, she said;
Her parents were alive - but where?
They could not be dead.

She pleaded to be taken home -
But who could know which home she meant?
This is her home,
Her home is here;
There is no other.

Now even her body fails her.
Her feet grope for the stair
And fail to find it.
Slowly, slowly those who care for her
Guide her from room to room, from chair to chair.
Her body no longer knows its place.
Now, she still seems perplexed;
But the seeking eyes,
So beautiful a blue,
Ask an answerable question:
"Do you love me?"
Yes we do.
And the one remaining quality
Which is and always was Elizabeth
Looks from her eyes in simple clarity,
Saying, "I love you too."
                    Margaret Sparshott, February 2005.

MEMORIES ARE SAFE

There is no drowning
In this sea of sorrow; no,
It is a flowing from happiness of being
To something other,
Unsought, perhaps,
But full of other mysteries.
It is a different sea
From that of happy union,
But the unseen presence
Is the same, if we did but know it.
Memories of those we love
Are safe from violation,
Under the lock and key of our hearts.

Oh why are we so dependent
On eyes and ears and touch,
When deeper sense could show us
That we are not alone?

Margaret Sparshott, August, 2006
First Published in 'Count Our Blessings'
Forward Press 2007

John is *'The Woodsman'* of this next poem. The heath
and broadleaf woodland he has replanted and restored are in
Surrey. Some of them are now mature, but some are still in the
early stages of growth, and he will never see them as forest.
The wood in this poem is the first he and Elizabeth ever
bought.

John has also transformed part of Brittany, restoring an
old water mill, and clearing the stream. He created a green ride
around this property called 'Ladywalk' and indeed Elizabeth
loved to walk there; it passed a bank of rare wild orchids.

THE WOODSMAN

It is a year ago now since his wife died.
He was beside her as she eased out of life,
Each slow breath taking her,
Further and further, over the summit.
Did he believe her last breath
Took her away from him?
Did it seem as if all that was left
Was a long silence?

But then he remembered all the trees planted
That she would watch grow.
He remembered their first wood,
And the hut from which they looked out on
Trees.
They heard the hush of young leaves stirring
When spring clothed the branches.
They saw the shameless nakedness of winter
Daring to bare all in beauty.
Behind the hut at dusk
They would watch badgers,
See deer shadow the glade, and hear -
Oh! An orchestra of birds!
She loved to hear the birds.

Now he has planted many woods,
Oaks and beeches, cherry and wild pear –
Acres of heath, where the Warblers
Proclaim their ownership.
They are all flourishing because
He created them with care.
He will never see all of them grow.

He has given the world a gift that he will not receive.
These woods, the sandy paths,
The green rides,
Will delight the eyes
Of people he will never know.
The benefit to him
Is to remember the pleasure she took in trees –
She loved them so.

Margaret Sparshott, November 2006

John and Elizabeth bought their first wood whilst I was still working in Greece; I used to see them from time to time when they came to Athens visiting friends.

Shortly after they bought the wood I came to visit them on holiday, and we went there together. It was a magical place and it reminded me of the following Greek song, which was popular at that time, *A Deep Silence Fell,* which was on the record *The Roadway* sung by Yannis Poulopoulos. I later brought the record home for them.

I am not entirely satisfied with this poem; it is hard to translate the sadness and strangeness of the imagery. It is of course quite impossible to catch the sorrow and beauty of the music, but I play the record still.

A DEEP SILENCE FELL

There fell a deep silence in our old wood;
"Run, and I'll catch you!" you said to me then.
And when rain spattered the fallen leaves
How it shivered through my soul!

Bitter yellow wine, yellow moon.
Taking you with them, the soldiers are gone;
And deep in your eyes I saw the gleam –
I saw the dark gleam of night's descent.

There bleeds a wound that will not heal
In the small church beside the well;
Now a bleak spirit haunts our wood.
How can I forget that earth has taken you?

Margaret Sparshott, 2006:
Translated from Lefteris Papadopoulos

This next poem tells of the musical evenings, which still happen at Green Farm; it recalls the music and a conversation we had during one of them.

THE MUSIC OF BIRDS

They play:
> These old instruments, violin, viol de gamba, recorder,
> and spinnet.

They play:
> And the cuckoo sings from the wood.

They play:
> And the lark sings from the airport runway.

They play:
> And the nightingale sings from the heart.

> *Margaret Sparshott:*
> *Green Farm May 2007*

'*File Not Found*' is one of the last poems I have written, all because a speaker at Lee Abbey asked us "Today and tomorrow, how do you want to live your life?"

FILE NOT FOUND

I sit at my computer.
It knows all.
It thinks it is my friend, so
I will put it to the test.

"Today and tomorrow,
How do I want to live my life?
I would like to enter the mind of Jesus,
Live as he lived, love as he loved,
Heal as he healed, die as he died –
Save as he saved."

Computer says: "File not found."

"I would like to live like Jesus
And be a friend to all;
How good to be a friend to all!
I would rush about with my disciples,
Teach them, guide them,
Watch them hang on every word,
Dependent, puzzled – lost;
See them at my feet … "

Computer says: "File not found."

"I would like to love as he loved;
Love the poor and the hungry,
The sinners and the good,

The sick, the sorrowful, the lonely;
Love father and mother,
Friends and followers –
Enemies, I would love them, too.
How I would love them!"

Computer says: "File not found."

"I would like to heal as he healed.
Oh, how I would lift the lame from the ground!
Touch blind eyes to wonder at my face!
Touch deaf ears to marvel at my voice!
Raise the unhappy dead . . ."

"File not found."

But would I like to die as he died,
Naked, wounded and alone,
Abandoned on the Cross?

I cannot die as Jesus died.
I cannot save as Jesus saved.
There is no mystic, magic word
To open that file.

My computer is not a friend,
It is only a computer;
It can tell me all it knows, but
It does not know everything.
It does not know me.
"Shall I shut down?" it asks.
"Yes," I reply,
"Shut down."

Margaret Sparshott,

Advent Retreat, Lee, November 2006

Twice a year, I go with other members of my church to pass a 'Quiet Day' at Hampton Manor, near Callington in Cornwall. These days are passed in beautiful surroundings, in community and silence, and are a source of refreshment to me and my hard working friends. I wrote this poem during a day in June, when I was suffering pain from a hip joint, which made it difficult for me to walk and stand for long.

HAMPTON MANOR

There is pain:
    But there is no telephone,
    No voices argue, pronounce, insist, beguile –
    No loved voice intrudes;
    Only birdsong, and the muted hum
    Of insects –
    These make no demands.

There is pain;
    But there is the touch
    Of the soft grass beneath my back,
    The feel of cool grass between fingers,
    Fallen twigs and fallen leaves –
    There is the scent
    Of herbs abundant –
    These make no demands.

There is pain;
    But as I look up,
    There is the beech tree above my head.
    I see green leaves against the sky,
    Pale in the sun, dark in the shade;
    I see

Silvery branches stirring
Against blue sky in June –
These make no demands.

There is pain;
But there is not only pain.
Perhaps the pain reminds me
That fed, unthreatened,
Here I lie at peace,
Beloved and loving,
Turning quietly
With the quietly turning world.

Margaret Sparshott,
Hampton Manor, June 2007

And all through these years, reading the poems and remembering how I felt in those far off days, I can now see that this has been – still is – a spiritual journey, which draws me closer to the God who loves all his neglectful children – who, incredibly, loves me. God's love is there for us all to rest on, and hard as it is to climb out of the fret of here and now - there I do rest.

INNER LIFE

Now is the time for silence;
But there will never be silence, not
While the humming of wires,
The rushing of streams
Keep alive this busy body.
Even in the silence of the night
Behind closed windows and doors –

Behind hands clasped over ears –
Sound the waves of an inner sea.

Now is the time for darkness
In the closed cellar of the night –
Behind hands clasped over eyes –
Now is the time to be blind.
But then I see the matt dark
Of a mind filled with circles and stars,
The slowly moving planets of my own
Created universe.

Never silent, never black,
This is the sound and vision
You, my Creator, have given me.
This is my own invisible sanctuary;
My passionately living, inmost,
Solitary world.

Margaret Sparshott, March, 2005

INDEX OF POEMS

INDEX AND NOTES ON THE DRAWINGS

speaker at Lee Abbey. The poem was inspired by the drawing.

Page 140   *The Road to Emmaus*
            Drawing created for the poem.

Page 145   *Sister Noname*
            It was early morning, and I saw this nun from a window at the Community of St. Francis at Compton Durville. It was a quick sketch, and not meant to be a portrait; the poem was written later.

Page 152   *Our Mother Died*
            Drawing from a photograph taken by my brother Francis.

Page 154   *Three Pairs of Hands*
            Design for the book cover of *Relating to the Relatives* by Thurstan Brewin, with Margaret Sparshott, published by Radcliffe Medical Press in 1996. It was never used, but the drawing gave me the idea for the poem.

Page 158   *The Table in Silence*
            I drew this scene from memory while it was still fresh in my mind. The poem was written later.

About the author

Margaret Sparshott trained as a general nurse at St. Thomas' Hospital London in 1955 and is also a trained midwife. After several years in general nursing in England, she worked abroad for twenty years as a neonatal nurse in Greece and Switzerland. She also spent nine months working for the International Committee of the Red Cross in Cyprus during the Turkish invasion, and was Assistant Director of Nursing at a private hospital in Geneva. In September 1986 she returned to England to a post as staff nurse on a neonatal intensive care unit in Plymouth, where she began researching the problem of newborn pain.

Margaret has lectured and written many articles on the environmental problems of the sick/preterm baby in hospital. She contributed to the book *'Relating to the Relatives: breaking bad news, communication and support'* published in 1996. Her own book *'Pain, Distress and the Newborn Baby'* was published in 1997. In 1991 she was the winner of the Nursing tmes/3M National Nursing Award for Practice and in 1998 and the three following years was a guest at the Women of the Year Lunch and Assembly at the Savoy Hotel, London.

After 45 years in the profession she retired from clinical nursing in June 1999. Now she has time to enjoy the pleasures of reading, writing, gardening and singing and she still loves travelling abroad. Margaret has used poetry to put into words the experiences of her professional and spiritual life.